Ben Tiggelaar

Dream, Dare, Do,

Managing the most difficult person on earth: yourself

Tyler Roland Press

First Published in 2008 by:
Tyler Roland Press, The Netherlands

www.tylerrolandpress.com
ISBN: 978-90-79445-01-1

First edition

Translation by Annerie Godschalk
Photo Ben Tiggelaar by Corb!no
Cover design by Bertil Merkus
Book design by Drukpunt B.V., Rijswijk
Printed and bound in The Netherlands by Drukpunt B.V., Rijswijk

Contents

To Ingrid, Maria, Isabelle, Emma and Bernice

Acknowledgments

The past few years I have been able to train thousands of people, sometimes in sessions with large groups, sometimes in individual meetings. The feedback I got from these people has been very valuable. Many topics, examples, and ideas were developed and formed during these sessions.

I thank Ingrid, my wife, who has always given down-to-earth and practical comments on my ideas; Nanja Tiggelaar, my sister, who did the interviews for this book and was a critical reader; Erna Kempen for her support and feedback; and my publisher for stimulating me to write this book.

Special thanks to all people who were willing to tell their personal stories in this book. (For privacy reasons, their names have been changed and will not be mentioned here either).

Sources

The core content of this book is based on personal research and a bookcase full of literature on the subject of behavior. The examples and tips are derived from my own experience, from talks with readers and from valued fellow-trainers.

Dream, Dare, Do

You have decided you would like to take more control of your own life. You even have some sense of direction. But you think it is going to be difficult. Maybe too difficult.

Don't worry. This book is going to help you.

My frustration

A multitude of books have been written about *what* you should manage or change in your life. Bookstores are filled with books with advice on relations, happiness, work, food, physical exercise, entrepreneurship, spiritualism, and so on.
But *how* this works exactly, *how* you can really make sure you turn this advice into practice, how you can get more grip on your own behavior.... this remains a dark secret to many people.

Many books end – after a long series of advice – with the simple statement that you just have to do it. '*Just*'....
Many other books suffice with 'open door' advice like: 'It is a matter of persevering and persisting.' Or vague language like: 'Listen to the voice of your soul.'
I have always persevered and followed the advice of my soul, but I have never had the impression it really helped. Absolutely frustrating.

All-purpose wipe
In the end change and growth are all about 'managing' your own behavior. That actually is the weak link between plans and results. We may know what we would like to achieve, we may know what we have to do to achieve this, but how can we motivate ourselves to start and really persevere. For many people – including me – that is the main problem.

In my previous book *Can Do!* I described in detail what this entails. Some people call the book an 'all-purpose wipe' for behavioral change. And in practice this appears to be so. I have received numerous letters and e-mails from people who have used the book in many different situations,

Managers let me know that they use it for changes in their company. Dieticians advised each other to use the methodology from *Can Do!* to help people lose weight. Entrepreneurs use the approach for self-motivation. A rehab center uses it to help its clients take control of their lives again. Parents use it to raise their kids.

In this book the same approach is followed as in *Can Do!* but in a more concise way, without technical terms and with new examples and many tips.

What this book will bring you
This book doesn't contain heavy reading material or vague language. I present a realistic, practical approach that really works. It is a bit like sports. There are a few rules for managing behavior, and it is sensible to practice a bit. But if you are taking it seriously it can deliver wonderful results.

You are already familiar with some of the things in this book. You are familiar with them, but you may not be applying them yet. And some things in this book will be new to you.

The first three chapters mainly deal with your behavior. You will get more insight into yourself. You will understand better how your behavior works and how you can change things.

In chapters four through to ten you will be presented with techniques with which to improve the management of your own behavior. Research has convincingly shown that these particular techniques lead to clear, and sometimes very powerful, effects.

Between chapters you will also find nine interviews with people who have made major changes in their lives. Real, honest stories of ordinary people who have experienced or done extraordinary things.

Ben Tiggelaar

1 The most difficult person on earth to deal with: you

- ***Do plans and intentions actually help?***
- ***Why you often do something you do not want to do (and the other way around)***
- ***Two kinds of opposing behavior***

A few years ago I weighed much too much. Something like that creeps upon you. A few years on end I ate at the better 'restaurants' when I was on the road for work. A snack at Shell's. Another one at Texaco's. An ice-cream cone at Esso's. All in all a rather unhealthy pattern of nutrition.
Of course I noticed that I gained weight, but by carefully avoiding the scales I could tell myself it was not that bad. Until, on a bad day, my wife bought electronic scales and dared me to stand on them. I appeared to weigh more than 240 pounds. A healthy weight would be 55 pounds lower. And about 33 pounds more than I assumed I weighed.

By carefully avoiding the scales I could tell myself it was not that bad

This kind of moment helps to get changes going.
You can tell yourself for a long time that in fact you eat too much and exercise too little. For a long time you can dream about a tight and healthy body. But something has to happen which makes you want to start changing. Something which motivates you to really *do* something.

This is actually weird. In our daily lives we do many things again and again, but we don't really want to do them. And we want to do a lot of things which we do not do. We exercise less than we should; we eat less healthy than we should; we invest less time in our loved ones than would be good, and so on.

'What I do, I do not understand. For I do not do what I want, but I do what I hate.' It looks like a complaint from any person from our day and age, but the quotation comes from the Bible (Romans 7:15) and is almost two thousand years old. There is nothing new under the sun.

Good intentions alone do not work

Managing yourself is difficult. Most people I meet are full of good intentions. So am I. Here is a small collection of the intentions I have heard in the workshops in the past few years:

- *I want to say 'no' more often to things I really do not want to do.*
- *I want to eat healthier food and exercise more.*
- *I want to give my relationship a boost.*
- *I want to be more confident.*
- *I have to learn to listen better to others.*
- *I have wanted to set up my own company for years.*
- *I don't experience peace of mind. I want to get the feeling that I contribute to something that really matters.*
- *I want to start studying again. I want to develop myself.*
- *I just want to go through life more positively.*
- *I have to stop constantly correcting others.*

The American researcher John Norcross has studied good intentions for years. He found out, as you might have suspected, that in most cases people do not manage to maintain their intentions.
For example, more than half of the people who start a change in their lives at the New Year have fallen back into their old habits by the month of July. And after two years only one out of five people appears to have persevered.

So the bad news is that good intentions alone do not help. Apparently you need more than saying your intention out loud to change something in your life.

The good news is that a concrete intention is not completely useless. Norcross also did research on the effect of just a wish to change and not a concrete behavior intention. It appeared that of those people not more than 4% had realized a change in their lives six months later. Ten times fewer than those people who translated their wishes into concrete behavior intentions.

Behavior is the weak link

The research into New Year's resolutions fits in with something psychologists have known for ages. If a wish to change is not translated meticulously into behavior necessary to realize this change, it doesn't help much.

Many people have a sneaking desire to one day become more assertive; to meet the perfect partner; to spend more time with their family; to set up their own company; etcetera. It may sound irritating, but the truth is that most of these people keep dreaming until it's too late.

Behavior is the weak link between plans and results. We will have to decide very concretely what we have to do today to really achieve the long-term results that we think are worthwhile. Everybody knows that a chain is as strong as its weakest link. And in many changes in our lives behavior is that weak link. Therefore, whoever wants to change something in his life and does want to move away from secret wishes, needs to concentrate on his behavior.

But what actually is behavior? Simply put, behavior is everything we do. All actions we take of our own accord or in reaction to our environment. Among them are our movements and our words (visible to the outside world) and our thoughts and feelings (invisible to others).

The truth is that most of these people keep dreaming until it's too late

Two types of behavior

Psychologists and other behavioral scientists delight in distinguishing themselves from each other. And so there are very different insights and opinions. But almost all psychologists agree on one thing: there are at least two types of behavior.
You and I and all other people on this planet do some things *con-*

sciously and *planned*. And we do other things *unconsciously* and *automatically*.

Sometimes we clearly discuss the future with ourselves or with others and form a concrete intention in our minds which we subsequently (sometimes) execute as well. We especially do this with behavior that occurs only once or a few times a year or even less. For example when planning a holiday or when choosing the person we are going to marry.

However, many behaviors are not consciously executed in our minds, but are effective behaviors from the past which are repeated fully *automatically*.
We don't consciously take notice of many of the actions we perform in traffic, for example. Fully automatically we keep a certain distance to the car in front of us. Meanwhile we look at the signposts and have a telephone conversation. We drive – almost literally – on automatic pilot.
These unconscious processes are especially part of behavior that we display weekly, daily or more often. Those automatic behaviors – habits – are the ones which are in the way when we want to make changes.

You can imagine two types of behavior like two parts of an iceberg. Conscious behavior is the part above water. It is what you 'see' in your mind. Unconscious behavior is the part beneath the water. You know it is there, for example when you read about it in a book, but you don't 'see' it in your mind.

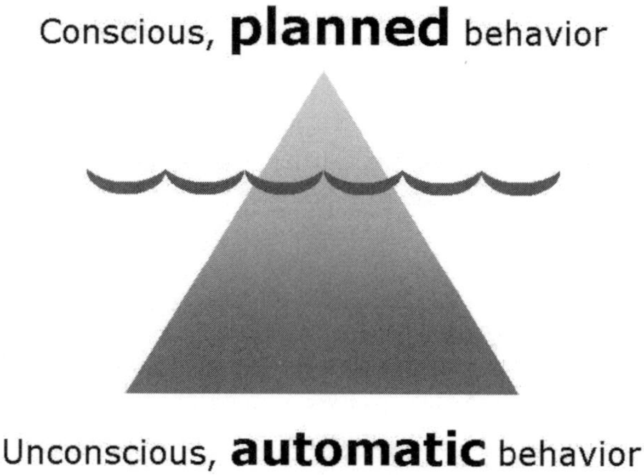

There are two types of behavior: conscious, planned behavior (5%) and unconscious, automatic behavior (95%).

Conscious, planned behavior (5%)
Let us start above water. Part of our behavior is the consequence of the plans we make. This behavior, which we discuss with ourselves in our minds, is called conscious, planned behavior.
We know beforehand what we want and subsequently also do it. At least, that is the idea. But we have already seen that often we don't succeed in actually putting our intentions into action.

According to American researcher Icek Ajzen, three factors play a major role in forming the intentions referred to.

1. *We estimate the use of our intended behavior.* During our lives we gather all kinds of beliefs about the use of certain behaviors. We have an opinion about the question whether running has an effect on losing weight; whether a romantic weekend has an effect on improving your relationship; whether going to the doctor is useful if you have the flu, etcetera.

Mind you: it isn't about whether the behavior is really useful, but only what we think about it.

2. *We consider what other people, who are important to us, will think about our intended behavior.* We have all kinds of thoughts about other people's opinion: 'My partner will probably think this not a bright idea'; 'My friends will laugh at me when I tell them.' Mind you: it is not what people really think, but what we think they think.

3. *Finally, we ask ourselves whether we are able to really put our intended behavior into action.* All kinds of beliefs we have about ourselves are involved here: 'I am just not a stayer in sports'; 'Fortunately, I am reasonably good at writing letters of application'; 'I am not very good at saying "no"'.
Mind you: again, this is not about whether we are really good or bad at something. It is about what we think about it.

According to most psychologists only a small part of our behavior is consciously chosen

Conscious, planned behavior is behavior we contemplate in our minds beforehand. We consider in our minds what is going to happen beforehand. And we especially do this when something is involved that we don't do very often: once or a few times per year.
According to most psychologists only a small part of our behavior is consciously chosen. It is estimated that this part is only 5% or smaller. But this is a very important part. Major choices in life, long-term decisions, are usually made consciously.

Unconscious, automatic behavior (95%)
Unconscious, automatic behavior is the kind of behavior which often amazes us, even if it is our own. Those are the things we do which we can't clearly remember. The kind of behavior which we display on automatic pilot.

I already gave the example of driving a car. We often drive for miles without knowing exactly where we have been, looking back. Sometimes we even get the feeling we 'wake up' behind the wheel. When we suddenly pass a landmark or when the situation suddenly requires our full attention.

Until that moment we have kept the car between the white lines and at a safe distance from other drivers fully automatically. We have reacted to all kinds of signals from our direct environment fully automatically. In fact we do not *drive* the car ourselves at such moments, but the car is driven by stimuli from the immediate environment, through our unconscious behavior.

Unconscious, automatic behavior largely determines the results we see in our lives. How you deal with your partner determines the quality of your relationship. And what you do at your work every day, to a large extent, determines how your career develops.

These daily habits also determine how other people perceive us. When others have to describe our character or our personality they usually mention those behaviors that we display automatically daily. This unconscious, automatic behavior determines the quality of our lives to a large extent. It is estimated that more than 95% of our behavior is brought about unconsciously and automatically. As this is unconscious behavior, it is also behavior that we usually know least about. That is why the next chapter is completely devoted to this.

What this means ....
As a rule our conscious, planned behavior is focused on things we don't often do and on achieving results in the future. We want to feel better in our bodies and we decide to start a healthy diet and exercise more. Those kinds of things.
Our unconscious, automatic behavior is steered by all kinds of stimuli in the here and now. We automatically resent behavior which immediately feels bad and have an automatic preference for behavior which immediately feels good.

You can imagine that these two types of behavior often clash. A healthier diet is a good plan in the long run, but in the short run it doesn't always feel good immediately.

More exercise really helps if we persevere for a few months, but the first few times we put on our jogging suits and run through the woods, it feels awful.

The annoying thing is that most behavioral changes only yield results in the long term. It sometimes costs months of daily repetitive behavior before we see results. This is especially true for the most important areas in our lives: relationship, personal development, health, and career.

Tearing something down usually doesn't cost so much effort. Misbehave once and you get instant results

Tearing something down usually doesn't cost so much effort. Ruining a friendship, flunking an exam, setting your colleagues against you. In fact this is all very easy to do. Misbehave once and you get instant results. But achieving positive results in areas in your life that really matter, almost always requires a long-term investment. Therefore, if you want to change something in your life, you will have to manage your conscious, planned behavior as well as your unconscious, automatic behavior!

Dream, Dare, Do ...

- Intentions alone are not sufficient to realize changes. Only one out of five people manages to maintain a good intention longer than two years.
- Behavior is the weak link between plans and results. Changes usually come to a standstill because we fail to change our behavior permanently.
- 5% of our behavior is brought about consciously and planned. 95%, however, is unconscious and automatic. It is exactly this type of behavior that makes changing so difficult.

'Apparently, I needed a crisis to be able to change'

Sarah (34): full-time working mom of nine-year-old triplets and a four-year-old daughter. Her husband works part-time. The past nine years the only thing they have actually done was run, run and run. Everything needed to be done fast.
Until Sarah realized that she was tired all of the time and didn't enjoy anything anymore. She didn't enjoy her kids, didn't enjoy her husband, didn't enjoy her work and she didn't enjoy herself. At the consultants' where she worked she had taken over tasks from the managing director, next to her own duties as HRM manager.
Everything combined, it was much too much. 'I was really at the end of my tether, but it took me a long while before I realized this. 'In the end, her children's remarks were the deciding factor. 'If your child tells the teacher that you can't help out at school because "mum is always at work", you suddenly clearly realize how she sees you.'

Realizing changes started by saying things out loud. First to people who she didn't have an emotional bond with; at a seminar and to a coach she already had. And after that to her husband. He was the one who got the ball rolling.
Sarah was almost ready to leave her home and family, but her husband refused to give up on her and pointed out her own part in this situation. This meant that she herself could influence the situation.
'He told me that he would support me whenever and wherever was necessary, but that I should start the process. Apparently I needed a crisis to be able to change.'

At that same moment it became clear that one of their daughters suffered from ADHD. This forced them to bring more structure into their lives. In a family where everybody is always running around, a child like that is at her wit's end. That is why there are weekly calendars on the fridge now. One with the children's activities, and one with Sarah's and her husband's activities. Sarah realizes that this makes things much clearer. They started making these calendars for their daughter, but in the end the system brings more peace for everybody. 'At first I really disliked being tied down to this structure, but when I saw that it worked I quickly turned around.'

'Now I mainly persevere because I see what I get in return'

They have also added more periods of rest. On Sunday night, for example, the children go to bed early. Sarah and her husband cook and have dinner together.
On Sunday during the day it is family day. This means not visiting relatives but doing things just with the six of them. It feels good and brings a lot of peace. In this way, they have made more time to do things together and they have cancelled as many commitments as possible. Other people's reactions to this were not always positive, but by being honest and consistent about what you want and what you do not want you can make things clear. At work Sarah indicated that she only wanted to do her own work and this has been realized as well.

'I have to force myself to persist. I often start very enthusiastically and then lose interest again. It costs time and energy before you can reap the benefits of your changes. Because I have made arrangements with my family I can persevere. My husband is very consistent. And the children have got used to the whole system as well. In fact, they got used to the arrangements we made and the new situation more quickly than I did.
It clearly is an interaction between me, the children, and my husband, and it is a continuous process. Now I mainly persevere because I see what I get in return. I am a much happier person now.'

Dream, Dare, Do ...

- Change starts with you. You are responsible for your own behavior and consequently also for changing it.
- Often a painful confrontation with reality is necessary to start thinking seriously about changing.
- Ask for help. You need people to make arrangements with and who will remind you of them. Also when this is difficult.

2 What you do not know that you do (but do anyway)

- ***What is the source of our habits?***
- ***How pleasure and pain determine our behavior***
- ***Why we are less rational than we thought***

Some time ago I talked to the company psychologist of a public transport company in a large city. 'You know,' he said, 'bus drivers regularly do funny things when they go into town in their own cars on the weekends.'
'Funny things?' I asked. 'Like driving on the bus lane?'
'That does happen but they do even stranger things. Bus drivers regularly tend to stop with their own cars at bus stops on the weekends. Some of them really stop and – even weirder – they only realize this when they have come to a standstill.'

Most drivers are shocked when this happens to them. Some of them report to the company psychologist the next Monday and are afraid their work slowly drives them crazy. He can set heir minds at rest though. What happens to them is actually very normal.
'It is conditioning,' according to the psychologist. 'A stimulus or *condition* in the immediate environment leads to fully automatic behavior at a certain moment. During the working week this is very convenient. But on the weekends this sometimes causes funny situations.'

The Belgian endive effect

Another form of fully automatic behavior. Many people have a problem with a certain type of food – just ask anyone you know. If they have once eaten something in bad circumstances (for example on a rocking ferry, or during a time of illness), which caused them to throw up immediately, there is fair chance they don't eat this food for many years after.

In psychological terms this is called *taste aversion*. During a seminar I met a man who is most likely to be the European record holder in this area. When he was four he was forced to eat Belgian endive in hospital. The nurse who took care of him pinched his nose and literally forced the food in. He had to throw up immediately.
The man said: 'I am now seventy-five, but when people at the next table in a restaurant order Belgian endive, I still always ask the waiter to be seated somewhere else. I have been disgusted by it for more than seventy years now.'

This is also a form of conditioning. We eat something and immediately a severe, painful stimulus follows. Our brain makes a link which we can't get rid of for the rest of our lives.

How are habits formed?

The way automatic behavior works is similar to the working of an old-fashioned jukebox, or – to use a more modern version – the working of an MP3 player. You press a button and a certain song is played automatically.

Just press the button and the behavior automatically follows

Our habits work the same way. A stimulus from the outside triggers our behavior. The bus driver sees a specific sign in the right corner of his eye and fully automatically he plays the program with which he pulls over. Just press the button and the behavior automatically follows.

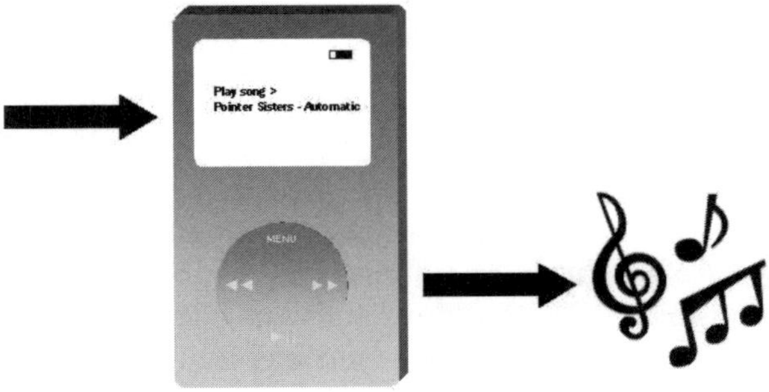

It is like the working of an MP3 player. You press a button and behavior is automatically (dis)played.

But you could ask yourself how this song gets into this jukebox or MP3 player. This doesn't happen automatically, does it?

This can happen in several ways.

- The most important way in which we learn new behavior is by *direct experience*. We try out all kinds of things. Some of them work, some of them do not. We store these experiences in our minds and when we meet comparable circumstances, the behavior that goes with these situations is displayed again.
- But we can also learn by *imagined experience*. We fantasize about how we are going to solve a problem at work, about how we are going to have this conversation with our partners, etcetera. It is true, this is less forceful than the real direct experience, but it also leads to new songs in the player.
- Finally we can learn something from other people's experience. By watching when others demonstrate something and by listening to

them when they explain. We learn from others at school, at work, in our family, on TV, through books, newspapers, radio, from movies. This form of learning is also less forceful than learning through own direct experience, but again new songs are added to our MP3 player.

Pleasure and pain

What causes a certain song in the MP3 player to become a hit or determines that it will never be played again? How does certain behavior become a habit, an automatism?

In fact, the answer is very simple. Behavior that *immediately* leads to a good feeling for us – pleasure – becomes a hit. And behavior that *immediately* leads to a bad feeling – pain – does not become a hit.

Pleasure and pain, reward and punishment, feeling good and feeling bad...Unconscious, automatic behavior increases when we can avoid pain and get pleasure. Unconscious, automatic behavior decreases when it doesn't yield anything or, even worse, causes pain.

Pleasure and pain are 'big' words. In practice, very small signals may be involved. Somebody looks at us friendly when we enter a shop. We experience that as a reward. Or somebody looks at us in a 'strange' way when we ask a question. We experience that as punishment.

It only works when punishment or reward immediately follows the behavior displayed. Otherwise our brain finds it too difficult to make the connection. Rewards which follow a few hours after certain behavior are not linked to each other by our brain.

A simple example: if you exercise actively for weeks on end to lose a few pounds, your brain clearly registers the link between exercising and the pain it costs. The link between exercising and losing weight is registered as a very vague one. That is why you can intuitively hate behavior which is very good for you for a long time, even if you see real results.

Also 'intelligent' behavior is conditioned

If stimuli from the immediate environment control our behavior, we call it conditioning. Literally this means that conditions in our environment determine what we do.

You can distinguish between two kinds of conditions or stimuli.

- Stimuli preceding behavior: a signal to our brain to start certain behavior. Remember the sign at the bus stop.
- Stimuli which follow behavior: pleasure or pain immediately after the behavior forms the signal to our brain to repeat certain songs or behaviors again and again or, on the contrary, not to (dis)play them that many times. Remember throwing up after eating contaminated food.

Most people think that conditioning only applies to 'simple' behavior. But this is certainly not the case. Read the text below:

This is the jukebox or MP3 player in full operation! Press the buttons a few times and, there you are, the behavior appears. A few stimuli from the outside and your brain shouts 'Cambridge'.
If you would like, you can stop yourself pronouncing the word. But you can't stop your brain from playing the song in your head.

This is a peculiar side of conditioning: *you can't stop it!*
At the very least you experience the urge to display certain behavior.

And if you do not consciously stop it you will fully automatically do these things.
Moreover: the songs are usually stuck in your MP3 player for years. And if we play them every now and again or if the songs lead to strong pleasure or pain stimuli (remember the Belgian endive effect) they will never disappear.

Automatic beliefs
Also the expectations we have, the prejudices, the automatic premonitions, the feelings of sympathy for one person, the feelings of antipathy towards another… in short*: the beliefs which control our thoughts to a large extent* mostly arise from the direct experiences we gain in our lives.

You apply for a job with a company and your looks and posture are a bit similar to the former math teacher of the personnel manager

An example: you apply for a job with a company and your looks and posture are a bit similar to the former math teacher of the personnel manager. This happens to be the teacher who abused him psychologically during his high school days. You will not stand a chance to get this job from the very start.
Even if you can answer all the questions in the right way and score the highest results on all tests, this personnel manager will never have the feeling he clicks with you.

Sometimes conditioning is a very handy thing. During the week the bus drivers pull over at the bus stops fully automatically and can pay attention to other, more important matters.
And sometimes conditioning is a real nuisance. For example, when on the weekend you stop at the bus stop with your own car, while your children laugh themselves silly in the back seat.

Which comes first: intention or behavior?
Many people think that we usually want something first and then take action. And finally – that is how they think – after a number of these planned, consciously chosen actions we will develop a habit.
But psychological research has shown that it can work the other way around as well. If we try out new behavior and this new behavior leads to pleasant, direct results, a conscious intention will be developed to repeat this behavior. In that case belief follows behavior.

Suppose you are on holiday abroad. In the restaurant the waiter advises you to take the surprise menu. One of the courses is something you have never had before, but it is delicious. The next time in another restaurant you remember this dish and you try to find the same food on the menu and maybe you decide to take the same dish again. Or – another possibility – you decide to be surprised once again because the previous surprise was such a nice one.

In fact, we know all this. For example, I strongly believe it is important that women get as many opportunities as men. Could this at all be related to the fact that I have four daughters full of life and ambition?

But it goes much further. When I am on my bike I usually think motorists don't show enough consideration for cyclists. And when I am at the wheel of my car, I usually think cyclists take too much space for their hobby. Sounds familiar?

How rational are we really?

After reading this story you may think: 'It looks like many of our 'rational' thoughts are a translation into words of our gut feeling. Are many of these arguments and discussions not just smooth translations of our first automatic reactions?'

Personally I think that many discussions – with ourselves and others – take place like this. We discuss by intuition, without wondering where this intuition comes from. And, as we have seen, this intuition can sometimes be a very good counselor and sometimes a very bad one.

When we have decided to change something in our lives and we need to change our habits – and believe you me, in most cases there is no escape from it – we will have to go against our old feelings in the first instance. The first few weeks and sometimes even months we will have to do things which didn't feel good up till then, which even hurt.

This is precisely what often makes changing so hard. This is precisely why many people prefer to stick to their old, ineffective habits, rather than make a start with a new, good life style which yields better results in the long term.

We discuss by intuition, without wondering where this intuition comes from

Fortunately, there are smart techniques with which we can in fact fool our own brain. We can make sure that the songs in the MP3 player which are good for us, but mainly caused us pain up till now, are linked to pleasure nevertheless. So we can condition ourselves in the right direction. I will refer to this later.

Dream, Dare, Do...

- Automatic behavior works like an MP3 player. After one or more stimuli from our environment – a button being pressed – behavior automatically follows.
- Behavior that immediately leads to pleasant consequences automatically increases. Behavior that immediately leads to negative consequences automatically decreases.
- In many cases, also 'intelligent' behavior is conditioned. Many of our expectations and prejudices are formed on the basis of one or more of experiences.

'Each night we check the score'

Peter (40), married to Carla, is a father of three children aged twelve, ten and five. For a long time he tried to 'manage' his children, in the same way most people do. On the one hand by giving compliments and rewarding, and on the other hand by making corrective remarks.
He was not very successful. Usually attention was given to things which didn't go well or were not done right, but little attention was given to the many things that went right. This led to numerous discussions.

During his holidays Peter read the book *Can Do!* and he started thinking about applying the strategies to his own family. To try and realize a change in behavior in his own family. 'I soon figured out how to do this and discussed it with my wife when we came back home. The next day we explained the idea to our children. They didn't get the raise in pocket money they had asked for but could earn a *lot more* on the basis of a scoring system. The kids could indicate what they would like to get if it were up to them: toys, going to the movies, McDonalds, etcetera. They wrote down all kinds of things and we attached a score to each suggestion. In this way we drew up a list of their wishes and added the number of credits they needed to score for each of them. Again, we discussed this list with our children.'

'I have become more aware of my own behavior'

'Of course their first question was how to score the credits. We told them it was very simple really. "All you need to do is brush your teeth for one credit. And if you make your bed, you will get another credit." Then they came up with all kind of ideas. Taking a shower, feeding the pets, buckling up in the car. And we awarded a high score for chores like mowing the lawn and doing some shopping. With these chores you can earn more credits but they are not compulsory. Each night after dinner we check the score.'

The credit system works, and they use it until this very day. 'After two weeks we started slacking off. And at moments they exchanged their credits for a prize it was difficult for them to start anew. We therefore agreed they had to keep a minimum score of five hundred credits so they would never reach a zero level. The whole system of positive reinforcement worked surprisingly well. You focus on what goes right instead of what goes wrong. The atmosphere at home is much better now because we don't have that many discussions on these topics anymore.'

Of course there will always be days when things don't run so smoothly. 'In the beginning we tended to react to this. Self control is of the utmost importance in these situations. You give your children the possibility to make choices. You really have to leave those choices up to them. Now we give certain incentives when a chore tends to be "forgotten". If one of the kids for example doesn't make his bed we award a double bonus to the beds. This really works. We tried quitting the system for a month and quite a few things had become automatic like brushing the teeth. But other things were not done anymore, like setting the table. That had not turned into a habit. But some things you may never learn. I myself am not very good at setting the table either.'

Peter noticed that he had to adapt his own behavior as well. 'I guess that was the most difficult part. In first instance, we figured we would not really be involved in these changes. And then you notice that your children expect something from you in return as well. As an example: I can't afford not to buckle up anymore. I have become more aware of my own behavior and the example I set.'

Dream, Dare, Do ...

- We tend to react especially to things that don't go right. This regularly leads to discussions and conflicts.
- If you want to change something together with your family or others you should involve them actively in developing the system.
- Measuring and rewarding have an immediate effect. This is a valuable approach, especially for behavior which is not 'automatically' considered nice.

3 'Surprise': losses count double

- ***The remarkable imbalance between pleasure and pain***
- ***What are the side effects of punishments as 'management techniques'?***
- ***Why rewards work better in the end***

When our fourth child was on its way, my wife and I decided, it would be fun to have a so-called fetal wellbeing scan made. An ultrasound scan during which we could take the time to see our unborn child in action.
I experienced this as very special. As a father you sometimes feel that you are not directly involved in the development of an unborn child, because you don't constantly feel his or her presence. It has a very large impact to see your child so clearly.

The sonographer told us a story that reminded me of the topic of this very book. She let us listen to the sound that the child had been hearing for months, day in and day out: the beat of my wife's heart. A steady rhythm sometimes rising to about one hundred and thirty, but usually about eighty beats per minute. 'This is what your child hears all these months. And when it is born, this sound has suddenly disappeared. Then there is light and all kinds of impressions come to him or her. No wonder a baby starts crying immediately. And when you want to quieten it, you only need one thing. You hold the child against its mother's breast. And as soon as it hears the steady heartbeat, again the child feels safe and becomes quiet'.

The dislike of loss

It is often claimed that people dislike changes by nature. This isn't true. People don't dislike changes, they dislike loss.

If a change immediately leads to progress in our situation without taking too much effort, pain, or loss, nobody complains. However, if a change leads to a better situation in the long term, but first requires a personal investment – time, money, energy, attention or giving up certain securities – it becomes a difficult matter.

People don't dislike changes, they dislike loss

Daniel Kahneman is one of the first researchers who described this phenomenon in detail. He calls it *loss aversion*. Loss aversion is innate to all people. Whether you are an Eskimo, an Aboriginal, a European or an American, on average loss hits us twice as hard as a rationally comparable reward.

For example, if we can earn one hundred dollars, we are prepared to run a mile for them. But if we are in danger of losing these same one hundred dollars, we are willing to walk as many as two and a half miles to keep our money.

According to many researchers, there is a direct connection with our instinct for survival. Danger and threats form much stronger stimuli for living creatures like you and me as they make our chance of survival larger. Sounds logical.

Understanding

When I first encountered Kahneman's research a lot of things fell into place for me.

- I understood why people can suddenly become motivated for a change if they are confronted with a threat.
  I once met a man who quit smoking from one day to the next without any effort as his doctor told him his legs should be amputated if he didn't stop *immediately*.
- I also understood why so many people become motivated to *oppose* changes. For example, changes in the company they work in or which are assigned by politicians. Often such changes bring long-term gains for many people, but require giving up certain things by certain people in the short term, such as security, acquired rights, time, money, jobs, status.

Let's be honest: this is also the way it works for individual changes. In the long run you might look better if you eat healthier and exercise more, but here and now you definitely lose a few things you like very much.
In the long run studying and applying for another job may lead to a nice new job. But in the here and now you lose a lot of spare time for sure, and at job interviews you will certainly have to deal with personal rejections. Rationally, consciously planned, it is sensible to make this investment. Intuitively, unconsciously, it feels wrong to give up all good things to this end.

Remarkable
You may have learned from a course or a book on 'positive thinking' that you should not think in terms of *problems* but should translate everything immediately into *challenges* and *opportunities*. Well, this is not true!
The motivating force of a real problem is much bigger than the motivating force of an opportunity. On the contrary, it is much more effective to wonder at each opportunity that you see which problem you can solve with it. At once, your motivation is twice to two and a half times as high.
I am saying this in jest, but am nevertheless serious about it. The fact that punishments and threats carry more weight than rewards and opportunities leads to all sorts of strange effects.

One of them is that it is very difficult to be and stay motivated if there are no *real* problems. In the opening chapter of this book I wrote that I weighed 55 pounds too many a few years ago. Meanwhile, I have lost more than 50 pounds with techniques I will describe in chapters four through to ten.
By changing my eating behavior permanently in a number of ways it is not so difficult to maintain my current weight. But to lose the last few pounds is very hard. Let us be honest: five pounds too many is a completely different story than 55 pounds too many.

'Good is the enemy of great', the American researcher Jim Collins wrote. And that is exactly the way it is.

This explains why so many people relapse into their old habits when they have reached their goals after a temporary effort.
Whether this is losing weight, working on your career, investing in your relationship or working on self-improvement...As soon as the acute, serious, real problems have disappeared below the horizon the motivation disappears and we tend to take things easy again.

Another remarkable effect
Another remarkable effect: as pain and loss hit us so hard, punishments and threats by others have such a powerful effect. That is why we tend to make use of these methods to an exaggerated extent in the education of children and sometimes also in the contacts with other adults.

I punish the little people and tell them what horrible things will happen

And when especially do we make use of threats and punishments? Exactly! When we stand to lose something ourselves.

A good example are my attempts to work from home while I take care of my daughters. How does this work? I am at the kitchen table with my laptop. I try to make a few calls, to write and to do some e-mails. Meanwhile my children are playing. As long as this goes well I don't pay any attention to them. This is only logical; I try to finish as many of my tasks as possible. But as soon as I am interrupted in my work, because, for example the girls start quarreling, I step in. I punish the little people and tell them what horrible things will happen if they continue like this. Usually this works immediately, and I can continue working, at least for a while.

I could also reward the foursome at those moments they are playing nicely and quietly. That would somewhat increase the chance for me to be able to continue working in peace. But I don't do this. Namely, in order to do this, I need to interrupt my own work and that feels like losing.
When I finally am interrupted by their behavior I do step in, because I do want to continue the task I was engaged in.

Moreover: my threat or punishment immediately has a much more powerful effect (factor two and a half) on their behavior. So I can immediately continue my work.

Meanwhile my brain has made the link: punishing the children immediately leads to positive consequences for me. Rewarding the children, on the other hand, will *cost* me immediately. *Consequence: intuitively, automatically I develop a preference for punishment as an educational method!*

Why punishment does not work in the long run

Punishments and threats work excellently when managing yourself and others. But only in the short run. And what is more, there are a few disadvantages.

First of all, people tend to do exactly what is required from them under threat, but not an inch more.

When I am able to convince my children they should clean up the mess in their rooms under powerful threats it usually looks tidy on the face of it. But when I open any of the closets the mess falls out. That is only logical. Their only goal was avoiding punishment, not winning a prize for the tidiest room.

In addition we tend to only adapt our behavior when a threat comes close. I call this the *speed camera effect*. Look at how it works in those places where a camera is placed at the side of the road. Motorists approach at a speed of so many miles per hour, drive like a good boy or girl for a while and subsequently put their foot down again.

Some people agree to weigh weekly in the presence of others. They hope this will motivate them to lose weight. Usually the consequence is that they only watch their behavior a few days before weighing and in the few days after the weighing much less.

And people, who 'motivate' their colleagues by threatening them with all kinds of horrible things lose their authority as soon as they have closed the door behind them.

People, who 'motivate' by threatening lose their authority as soon as they have closed the door behind them

In the end using punishments and threats a lot will lead to disturbed relationships. As a rule, people don't associate a punishment or a threat with their own behavior, but with the person who deals out punishment or utters threats.

At the moment that it really matters it may appear that you have lost all your credit. And even your loved ones get a 'Belgian endive' feeling (remember the incident of developing an aversion for a certain type of food) when you enter the room.

Just to make myself clear: by punishments and threats I don't only mean large gestures and forceful expressions. A disapproving look, a deep sigh and turning the eyes to the ceiling, are clear enough for the receiver and can hit just as hard.

Rewards are better

When we are rewarded for our behavior our brain creates a link between the behavior and the reward. This causes an automatic tendency to display this behavior more often. Mind you: it is *not* a conscious choice for a reward, not a consideration like: *'Hmm, I get a reward for this behavior. You know what, I will display this behavior more often.'* That is not how it works.

A simple illustration of this is the way you can help young children to stop wetting their beds. Quite generally a method is applied nowadays whereby children are rewarded for their dry nights. Some parents work with stickers, others with small presents, yet others with fun activities. The surprising thing is that in most cases the children have stopped wetting their beds within a few days. So the link between the reward and the desired behavior even works in a child's sleep.

Behavioral researchers have known from the sixties that rewarding the desired behavior will ultimately lead to much better effects than punishing the undesired behavior. Positive reinforcement, as rewarding desired behavior is also called, has got a few nice characteristics.
Rather than returning to old undesired behavior when threats and punishments stop, we continue the desired behavior when we are given positive reinforcement. In theory – and sometimes in practice as well – we display the desired behavior until we have reached our limits.

There are, however, a few rules for rewarding.

- Rewarding has to take place during or immediately after the desired behavior. If you wait too long to give the reward, it isn't connected to the right behavior anymore.

- Rewards are custom-made. A compliment or a material reward (a present or money) is only a real reward if the receiver feels rewarded.
- If someone has independently chosen a certain action because he or she just likes doing it, disproportionate material rewards can undermine this free choice. There is a chance that the person will only continue to do it for the material reward.
- Social rewards, like compliments, don't create this problem. They are free and besides they are good for the mutual understanding between people.

A person who has rewarded somebody three times and has punished once, is back to square one

Four to one

Positive reinforcement also has the advantage of being good for the relationship. Although we tend to link rewards for behavior mainly to what we have done, it will not harm our attitude towards the person who rewards us either.

So when we reward ourselves or others for desired behavior, it will automatically lead to a more pleasant relationship. According to some behavioral researchers we only really work on a relationship with others if we manage to maintain a ratio between rewards and punishments of four to one. In other words: a person who has rewarded somebody three times and has punished once, is back to square one again. A person who has rewarded somebody four times and punished once, has made a small progress in the relationship.

We only really improve on a relationship if the ratio between reward and punishment is a minimum of four to one.

I have already told you about my adventures of working from home. When I first heard about this four to one rule, I recorded this ratio in the situation between my children and me one afternoon. Unfortunately, the ratio was closer to four punishments to one reward instead of the other way around. I had to conclude that combining work and care didn't do the relationship with my children any good.

Some time ago, there was somebody at the Department of Transportation who came up with the idea that it was better to reward motorists for good behavior than punishing them for breaking the law. Bonus credits if you did not exceed the 25-mile speed limit in the town center, instead of being caught at 30 miles per hour. He wanted to have a system installed in a few people's cars. This system would register their driving.

His idea failed to gain approval. 'Have they gone completely berserk?' said a Member of Parliament. 'You don't reward a thief for not breaking in, do you?'
'Adjusting your driving for a present? I wonder if people would do so. On the contrary, we have to increase the chance of arrest of offenders.'
Often we don't want to believe that rewarding is more effective in the end. This is only logical, as from our own observation it will always become clear that punishments are more effective. That is: if we don't really think about it.

Dream, Dare, Do...

- People do not hate changing, but they do hate losing. A threatening loss affects us two to two and a half times as much as an opportunity.
- Still, threats and punishments do not work in the long run. They don't lead to optimum achievements. They only work under supervision. And they are disruptive to relationships.
- Rewarding does not have any negative side effects. Rewarding four times as much as punishing or threatening is a safe norm in managing yourself and others.

'I knew I would not live long with my weight'

Ida (28) decided to change her life style rigorously and subsequently lost 163 pounds in one year. She went from 330 pounds to 167 pounds. From childhood, she had been plump and in fact, she had always been trying to lose weight. She did this especially for others and not because she really wanted to. She lacked the right motivation. Until, as she herself says, she saw the light.

'At a certain moment something just snapped. I knew I wanted to grow old, but with this weight, I would not live very long. I just had to take better care of myself.'
In first instance, Ida decided that she wanted to live a *healthier* life. She didn't have a clear immediate goal as to how many pounds she wanted to lose. Each pound lost was useful.

The first step was to join a sports club where she would feel comfortable. 'I joined a very small sports club with all types of people. Fat, thin, tall and short. I felt at ease there.
The very first time it became clear to me what I had put myself through. On the cross trainer I couldn't even keep going for five minutes. The next day I went there again, and again the day after. I've gone to the club now each day for one and a half years.'

Furthermore, Ida started a different and healthier diet. 'I really watched what I ate and counted the calories. At the beginning, I still craved for all kinds of unhealthy stuff but by choosing good healthy alternatives, I lost this urge after two months. As I had been trying to lose weight so many times before, I knew exactly what and how I should eat. Up till now, I just had not really applied what I knew. I lost weight quickly and had to buy some new clothes each week. Now I still have to get used to myself sometimes. I look in the mirror and am surprised at who I see.'

Eating healthier and exercising didn't cost that much effort. It was relatively easy to persevere because it delivered quick results. What did bother her were other people's reactions. 'People asked me whether I was ill, was I going to the sports club *again* and wasn't it time I stopped diet-

ing. And for the first time I heard how people had always thought about me when I weighed so much.
There were also people who suddenly asked me out or wanted to have a cup of coffee with me. Very weird.'

'I am still trying to find my balance. What can I eat and what not? I still check my weight every morning. This way I can see that I don't gain any weight and everything is ok. I hold on to seeing my weight and counting the calories regularly. This makes me feel secure. Next to that, it is important to stick to the healthy food and to keep exercising. In the end, this has given me so much energy and I never ever want to lose it again. And so I am not afraid it will go wrong again. I am stronger and happier, and feel a completely different person. I enjoy anything I do much more'

I still have to get used to myself sometimes

Dream, Dare, Do...

- We often *know* what is right for us, but we don't *do* it. Real changes are all about behavior and cost attention, time and energy.
- Find a new life style that suits you. Find good alternatives for old, ineffective habits. Important changes are not just for a little while – they are forever.
- Persevering is an art in itself. You should realize that sometimes you will have to keep measuring your behavior and results to retain your 'profit'.

4 Changing in phases: Dream, Dare, Do

- ***How successful changers deal with it***
- ***The three phases everybody goes through***
- ***From fast kicks to slow successes***

If you watch TV at night you enter the magical world of products which are not for sale in regular stores. In the months after the births of our children my wife and I regularly watched those programs around the time of the night feedings. We were amazed at the things which were offered through *Tell Sell* and other TV-stores, but at the same time we had a lot of fun watching the programs.

Usually these programs offer products which change your life without you having to go through any trouble at all. Reference is constantly made to the hope that you can become rich without working, gather knowledge without studying, and become fit without exercising.
Of course we would really like to believe all this. Even I grabbed the phone in the middle of the night to make a call. 'Ben, you are not really going to make that call, are you?,' my wife would say. 'But suppose it really works?' I would reply half asleep.

By nature we tend to choose the immediate satisfaction of our needs. And companies like *Tell Sell* (and others) take advantage of this. Because it works. It is successful. With this type of midnight commercial marathons a lot of money is made.
But if I am honest I have to admit that it doesn't work like this with

matters that really count in life. All things in my life which made me happy and grateful are things which either cost me blood, sweat and tears, or which were thrown into my lap without me having called a toll free number.

Changing takes place in phases

Almost all people who have realized a change in their lives successfully afterwards say: 'I should've done this much earlier!' This probably sounds very familiar.

On the other hand: almost everybody who starts an important change needs quite some time to ponder and think about it. If you really want to change something important in your life you will often have been working on this for many years in advance.

Step by step you approach the moment at which you decide take the plunge. Sometimes you do this without any specific cause. But often you are also confronted with a harsh reality which confirms what you expected about your health, your relationship, your happiness, your weight, or your career. You will find that in the interviews in this book such an external cause often plays an important part.

The American researcher James Prochaska has ascertained that people go through a number of phases when changing.

1. The phase before considering the change (precontemplation)
2. Considering the change (contemplation)
3. Preparing for the change (preparation)
4. Action
5. Maintenance

You sometimes hear people say you can only change when you are 'ready'. This is sort of true. Many change programs which are offered to help people lose weight for example don't appear to work, as Prochaska discovered. This is because they don't fit the phase in which people are at that moment.

If you are still *contemplating* a change in your life, it is of no use hiring a coach who only concentrates on *action*.

And if you want to take action it is extremely frustrating when you have bought a book which starts at the very beginning.

Dream, dare, do

This book is mainly concerned with the second up to and including the fifth phase from Prochaska's list. This is logical because if you were not contemplating a change in your life yet you would probably not have bought or borrowed this book.

- The *dream* phase is about contemplating the change and even some of its preparation
- The *dare* phase is completely about the preparation for the change
- The *do* phase is about action and maintenance

In this book we distinguish three phases:
the dream phase, the dare phase and the do phase.

I will tell you a bit more about it now, and in the following chapters I will give a step by step explanation.

The *dream* phase: We often know that we want to change something or experience a certain dissatisfaction about matters in our lives, but we don't yet exactly know what we want and what kind of behavior is necessary to achieve this.

In this phase we get to work together to make our dreams concrete. What is it we actually try to achieve? What direction do we wish to go? And what kind of behavior is necessary?

The purpose of this phase is *to formulate goal-oriented and concrete behavioral intentions.*

Many change programs don't work because they don't fit the phase in which people are at that moment

The *dare* phase: Many people think they know in advance that, no matter what, they will not succeed in changing their behavior. They know in advance that there will be crisis situations in which they will relapse into their old, ineffective habits. The very thought of this paralyzes them even before they have started.

But by making an overview of these situations and preparing for them with a few powerful change techniques, you increase your chances of success enormously.

The purpose of this phase is *to thoroughly prepare for the most difficult change situations.*

The *do* phase: Starting new behavior and maintaining it is usually not as easy as you would think. Not even when you have prepared matters thoroughly. The direct consequences of our new behavior, pleasure and pain, determine whether we continue or not.

By immediately measuring and rewarding your new behavior, you train your brain to turn this new behavior into a habit. The purpose of this phase is *to start, measure, reward, and maintain the desired behavior.*

Each phase will help you to further shape your change and to reinforce your self-control. But each step will take some effort and simultaneously be a test for your motivation!

In all three phases the focus is on *behavior*. To some psychologists it is so evident that changing is all about behavior that they hardly dare to mention this out loud. But in the many workshops I have given over the past years I noticed again and again that many people know which results they want to reach with a change, but insufficiently realize that a translation into concrete, practical behavior is necessary to actually achieve those results.

The core of my approach is to make sure your conscious intentions and automatic tendencies don't undermine, but actually reinforce each other.
Many long-term goals lead to short-term frustrations. We may be able to persevere for a while on willpower, but in an unguarded moment (for example when we are stressed or exhausted) our automatic pilot takes over and we relapse into our old, ineffective habits.
Therefore we mainly focus on unconscious, automatic behavior. The fact is, if you don't control your habits, they will control you!

Fast kicks
One of the things you have learned from chapter two is that our unconscious automatic behavior is mainly controlled by pleasure and pain stimuli which immediately follow the particular behavior. That is exactly what makes it so difficult for us to invest a lot of time and effort in a result which only is apparent in the long term.

In high school I always postponed studying for tests and exams until the very last moment. I could have started studying from the day I knew when the exam was going to take place. I could have divided the work into equal portions and reach the finish without stress. Only... I didn't do this. I *knew* it would've been better, but I didn't *feel* the need.

Only when the finish is in sight, when the reward or punishment comes closer, people's motivation increases and the final sprint is started. The special thing is that this is true for all people all over the world. Independent from race, culture or belief. It is an innate tendency which is inherent to the human species. And, by the way, also to most ape species. They also take their time with their chores in their natural environment and only make a sprint when they approach the finish line.
Our sensitivity to powerful stimuli in the short run sometimes leads to large problems. Addictions are developed in this way.
Drugs give us such strong rewards immediately, without delay, that our brain can't forget them. Besides, the fact that drugs have lost their effects after a while gives us a very unpleasant feeling. Craving for the reward you experienced earlier and fearing the threatening punishment, your

Only when the finish is in sight, people's motivation increases

brain urges your body to get new drugs. This is how it works with smoking, with drinking, with cocaine, but also with fast food and other 'innocent' addictions.
In fact, this is a nasty process. Drugs, and many other things which give you a kick immediately, first ruin your brain and subsequently ruin the rest of your life.

The approach in this book is aimed at surpassing this type of fast kicks and, on the contrary, realizing those things which require a somewhat longer effort. Things which lead to a more satisfactory result exactly because of this.
Consider how it works with love. Once a year making a final sprint when your partner's birthday is approaching isn't enough. Love requires a long-term daily maintenance. In addition, you will regularly have to overcome your own short-term interest.
Losing weight is always a good example. Losing a few pounds quickly leads to weighing more a year later than before our crash diet in more than ninety percent of the cases. Only if we manage to change our life style permanently, will we feel better permanently as well.

Slow successes
The most important changes in our lives are about overcoming our natural longing for fast fulfillment. These changes require overcoming of our innate and conditioned habits. Or, even better, they require us to break through our old, ineffective habits and acquire new, effective habits. You will probably not be surprised that this sometimes takes quite a lot of time and effort. If only because our current habits, even if they are bad for us in the long run, provide us with a sense of security. That is why habits are addictive.

The famous psychologist Carl Rogers thought that every person should at least learn two things in his life. Accepting a certain extent of insecurity and being able to postpone the reaping of rewards. Acquiring these two 'skills' can take a lifetime. It is a process of ups and downs, of growing older and wiser, of becoming an adult, sensible, maybe even wise, person.

What strikes me when you talk to wise, old people who have learned to accept sadness and insecurity, people who are capable of making their immediate shallow needs submissive to more important matters, is that they are not filled with unsatisfied desires. They have not acquired their adult attitude to life by sheer willpower and discipline. On the contrary, they have learned to genuinely enjoy this other way of living.

At the moment we decide to postpone or reject the immediate satisfaction of a shallow need, we can get an other immediate reward in return: the feeling that we have made the right choice. That we have done something right. A feeling of mastery.
At each change we realize in our lives we build this mastery. Slowly but surely we experience, despite the relative chaos life often is, that we can manage a few important things in our lives. We can manage our own goal-oriented behavior and the way in which we react to things we can't control.

Dream, Dare, Do...

- Changes go through several phases. The first, the *dream* phase, is about formulating goal-oriented and concrete behavioral intentions.
- The purpose of the second phase, the *dare* phase, is to prepare thoroughly for the most difficult moments of change. This is how we prevent relapsing into old, ineffective habits.
- The third phase is the *do* phase. Its purpose is to start measuring, rewarding and maintaining the desired behavior.

'Only after several talks with my doctor I understood I had a burn-out'

Family, fun and feeling good. Those are the three central values in **Robert's** life nowadays. A burn-out forced him to analyze what he really finds important in his life.
'I had been working on a large project for six years and was very ambitious and enthusiastic. I worked hard and loved it. After this project I was given a lot of other tasks from colleagues who couldn't do their own work anymore. I had to do my own work as well. At the same time the company was reorganized which increasingly gave me the feeling I had to justify my actions. I didn't have the feeling I was appreciated anymore.'

'In my opinion there was too much talking and too much time was wasted. And we didn't get around to the real work. I was really frustrated. I couldn't see things in the right perspective anymore and everything started to weigh heavier by the day. I was in my own way, but also in the way of the company culture.
Especially the last six months I was no longer able to sit still on the couch for five minutes. I was much too restless and felt guilty when I was not working.'

'The burn-out started quite innocently with tingling in my right arm, usually at night. After a few months the pain woke me up regularly. Until, suddenly, I couldn't even hold a pen anymore. The diagnosis was RSI. Not much later my left arm started bothering me as well, and I had trouble understanding e-mails. I felt everything was too much and I had to stay at home to take some rest for a few weeks.'

'But the symptoms became worse and worse. I got tingling and pain all over my body and had to keep moving to keep it bearable. The restlessness and irritation increased and I couldn't relax or sleep anymore. Then I found out I couldn't read or understand newspaper articles anymore. I also lost my way regularly and anxiety attacks started troubling me.
Only after several talks with my doctor it dawned on me that I had a burn-out. Something I had never expected of myself.'
'After I had been convinced that I had to take antidepressants things even became a bit worse for a while at first. Until, one morning, I woke up and saw everything mega-clearly. I wrote down what I thought, what

the bottlenecks were and started analyzing from there. With the help of medication I could think again and write down how the burn-out was caused, which characteristics played a role and what I really find important. In fact, those are only three things: family, fun and feeling good. Those have become the basis for everything. Also in my work. Work is still important but not as important as I thought.'

'Only three things are really important'

'Subsequently I set to work. I thought our house was too small for our temperamental family and started a home make-over.
I also thought it was important to make time for myself and exercise one fixed night a week. These are very concrete things you can organize yourself.
Feeling good also means taking time for the kids and my wife. Now I regularly take a day off and we do a fun thing together. Small things that I was not used to doing.'

A few months later Robert started working again very carefully. 'I threw away everything which was still on my desk, also my e-mails. This was a way for me to start with a clean slate. The first thing I did at work was to determine very clearly: what *do* I do, and what *don't* I do.
You need to make your framework very clear and communicate it. That isn't easy and also led to a few conflicts. It remains hard to manage your work environment.
All in all I have grown through this experience.
I have become more self-aware and my assertiveness has increased tremendously. And I have learned to let things go more easily, because I now know what is *really* important.'

Dream, Dare, Do...

- Sometimes it is not easy, but often it is necessary to know what you really find important in life. Take your time for that process.
- Set realistic objectives. Take matters you control as a starting point. Determine concretely what you will do and what you will not do.
- If a large change is necessary, it means you need to let go of the past. Don't keep looking back, but focus on the future and start with a clean slate.

5 Dream: deciding on your direction

- ***How do you decide what is worth striving for?***
- ***Being yourself more and still changing, how does that work?***
- ***What can you do with beliefs which stand in your way?***

I usually know quite well what I find important in life. When you ask me I will say things like: happiness, health, my family, peace. Yes, indeed, my parents raised me well.
But if you were to watch me for a few hours after having talked to me, you would see that I regularly get mad at others (especially in traffic), that I eat unhealthy food, that I spend a lot of time on my work, and that my family often has to wait for a while. These are the differences between conscious choices and unconscious behavior. We have discussed this earlier.

Fortunately, I sometimes actually do things which really match what I find important in life. Sometimes I have a day, an afternoon, or maybe even an hour in which there is a balance between what I really want and what I actually do. At these moments I am not somebody else. Then I am simply myself as well, but you could say my 'better self'.

In my opinion the secret of self-management, of change, personal growth (or whichever label you would like to use) is that you create more of these kinds of moments. *Don't become somebody else, but be more yourself as you are at your best moments.*

Nobody wants to become more himself as he is at his worst moments. Neither do you. But making two percent or more of this one percent of good moments is something I feel is very valuable. Something that the people I love will appreciate. And something I believe I can do. These are exactly the three requirements a good decision meets.

Be more yourself as you are at your best moments

Setting goals

Living goal-oriented is something many people are interested in. We want our lives to matter. We want to have a purpose in life.

On the other hand, I have noticed that for most people it is very difficult to just say in a few words what exactly this purpose in life is.

All those gurus and books which want me to formulate *The Ultimate Goal* in my life, *That One Dream* which makes life worthwhile, paralyze me rather than stimulate me.

But then again, some people wallow in the vaguely uncomfortable feeling that they have to change 'something' in their lives, but only a few try to find out what this 'something' is. That isn't very useful either. Whoever sets to work with powerful self-management techniques but doesn't have a sense of direction yet is like somebody who gets into a taxi and tells the driver to just drive around. 'It doesn't matter to me where I go'.

The popular British philosopher Alain de Botton said in an interview: 'To be happy you need to know yourself; understand what your needs are and whether they are realistic. So you need to think about yourself a lot. Only few people do this well as thinking is hard work. It tires you out.'

A sense of direction, some idea of what you do want to do and what you would like to avoid, is important. It is good to have a 'why' question as a starting point. A reason why you make an effort to actively manage your life in a few important areas.

But a tightly scheduled action plan which goes beyond your ninetieth birthday, is a bit exaggerated.

My advice is: keep it simple. Explore the things in your life which make you enthusiastic and the things in life which disappoint you. In other words: explore your YES area and your NO area, schedule a global plan. And get started!

Dream from a NO perspective

As punishment, threat and loss have such a large influence on our lives, you and I by nature tend to look at the negative elements in our lives more than at the things which do run smoothly.
Just open any newspaper. Bad news gets more attention than good news. Once every so many years somebody tries to get a 'good news' paper off the ground. In advance many people always say they think this is a splendid initiative, as so many horrible things are happening in the world. But after a while such a newspaper meets an inglorious end due to a lack of readers.

This focus on the NO area of our lives is a very convenient strategy for survival. And in many environments you can score with a critical attitude as well. But paying too much attention to the NO area hinders our development. It is too easy to be stuck in pessimism and a negative self-image.
Sometimes it is absolutely dangerous. Research into entrepreneurs who went bankrupt shows that in the months before their bankruptcies they usually didn't pay attention to successful matters, which could have saved them, but only paid attention to matters which went wrong in their companies.

These kinds of stories tend to remind me of rabbits. Rabbits which cross the road apparently watch the headlights of approaching cars until the moment they are run over. That isn't very smart. But, hey, they are rabbits after all. We humans should know better.

Rabbits which cross the road apparently watch the headlights of approaching cars until the moment they are run over

Does this mean the NO area is a no go area? Certainly not. Threatening problems can be an important motivation for change. We have discussed this in detail. It would not harm you to find out what kinds of problems are caused by bad habits. Imagine this as lively as you can.
It is only of the utmost importance not to get stuck in the NO area. Worries, problems and threatening losses should motivate us to arrive at solutions. And those solutions can be found in the YES area.

Dream from a YES perspective

The YES area is the total sum of your best moments until now.

Moments which even now still give you a good feeling when you think back to them. I am referring to those experiences which not only gave you a fast kick at that particular moment, but which have left deep marks in your life.

Our possibilities to further develop are stored in that YES area. It is in this area where we should search for solutions to the problems which come to us from the NO area.
Again: you don't have to spend all of your time in the YES area. The question, however, is: Which is more effective? Complaining for two hours on end? Or complaining for half an hour and looking for solutions for one and a half hours?

In Chapter one I said which three elements steer us by nature when our intentions are formed.

1. We want our intentions to be useful and important.
2. We would like other people who are important to us to approve of our intentions.
3. We have to believe that we have the possibilities to put our intentions into action.

These three items will help you when researching your YES area. It is a matter of posing the right questions, questions like these:

- What matters in your personal life are you grateful for? At what moments do you have that pleasant feeling that it all comes together?
- What activities can you do hours on end and love them?
- What things in society are you genuinely enthusiastic about? For which documentary, for example, do you stay up?
- What are the spiritual highlights in your life? At what moments did you have the feeling your life had real meaning?
- At what moments do you experience appreciation from the people who are dear to you?
- When do you notice you are good at something? During what kinds of activities, jobs, tasks do you feel that?

These questions are easier posed than answered. But, believe me, it is worthwhile spending some time on them.
When you have found a few tentative answers to these questions the

most important question of all may follow: the question which helps you to find your own direction.

Try to dream out loud: *what would life be like if these moments were not the exception, but the rule? Try to imagine this seriously and concretely.*

We often spend too much time on the NO area in our lives and too little time on the YES area.

A few dream suggestions

When you have listed your best moments, you will get some more sense of the direction which suits you. But if it is still rather vague you may want to use some of my suggestions below. Mind you, I don't mean to 'preach'. I rely on research by the American psychologist Martin Seligman. He is the founder of the Positive Psychology Center at the University of Pennsylvania. He recorded what things contribute objectively and measurably to people's happiness. In his list he distinguishes between 'circumstances' and 'virtues'.

The top five circumstances are as follows:

1. Living in a prosperous, democratic country
2. Maintaining an extensive social network
3. Being married

4. Believing in God
5. Avoiding negative emotions

Usually circumstances are the result of a series of efforts and can't simply be 'made'. Nor is this something you can do just 'temporarily'. On the other hand this list helps me to determine what is worthwhile striving for and what is not. It helps when choosing a direction.

Seligman also determined that some circumstances, which millions of people think make us happy, don't have any effect at all. Some of these are:
- Earning more money
- Moving to a warm country
- Staying healthy
- Getting the best possible education

These matters seem worthwhile, but, as a rule, they only provide a temporary boost. They create an intensified sense of happiness for a few months at the most. So you don't need to strive for them for a fulfillment of your life.

Seven virtues to dream of

Seligman points out that, next to circumstances which are worth striving for, there are also virtues which make life worthwhile. It is not for nothing that a number of rules of life recur in almost all major philosophies of life and religions. Many people experience that developing these virtues gives their lives life meaning and importance. From way back a distinction is made between four natural, human virtues and three spiritual or theological virtues.

Some circumstances, which millions of people think make us happy, don't have any effect at all

The four natural virtues are:
- Prudence (or wisdom): strive to act as wisely and sensibly as possible.
- Temperance (or self-control): take everything as far as is good and not any further.
- Justice: be honest and fair towards everyone.
- Fortitude (or perseverance): dare to make your own choices and stick to them.

These virtues can help you to get a clearer picture of what your YES area looks like. What were your moments of wisdom, self-control, justice and fortitude? What did you do? What did you think? And how did that feel?

The three spiritual virtues are:
- Faith: look for God and study His destiny for your life.
- Hope: trust God's promises.
- Love: love God above all things and love your neighbor like you love yourself.

These virtues will also help you to set meaningful goals in your life. I do, by the way, realize very well that the three spiritual virtues raise questions for many people. Some people have said goodbye to their religion much to their relief. They said goodbye to a church with all kinds of rules and little love and respect for people.

On the other hand I have personally experienced that a life without God can be a very empty life. If the definitive answer to my quest for meaning is that my life is completely meaningless and just a product of cosmic coincidence, this would be completely unsatisfactory to me.

You will understand that it is not about 'temporary, quick and easy' changes in this chapter. Just getting your shape and figure back before the summer, and those kinds of things.
These goals are not forbidden, of course not. But don't expect those things to make a real, permanent contribution to your happiness. More than that: temporary short-term goals almost always lead to quick relapses and corresponding frustration.

Self-defeating beliefs
If you do some research in your NO and YES area, for example on the basis of the circumstances which Seligman selected or from the point of view of the seven virtues, you will be able to determine your overall direction. You will be able to name what you think is important to strive for and what is not.

What strikes me is that a lot of people, once they know what they really find important in their lives, immediately see all kinds of obstacles for translating these insights into actual behavior.
They don't dare to trust that the direction they would like to choose for their lives is really the right one. Now, some caution isn't that bad of course, but often we stick to all kinds of old, self-defeating beliefs.

Beliefs like:
- I have no right to this; what I want is exaggerated; it may even be dangerous what I want; this is not my lot in life.
- Other people don't like me or this plan; no one will help me anyway.
- I will never be able to realize this; I will never be able to do it perfectly; I am not a go-getter; I am never going to make it.

You can regard beliefs as 'thoughts of habit'. Those are things that we normally believe about a certain topic. Those are the first words, images and other thoughts which the MP3 player puts into your mind automatically, when you are confronted with something: with an intention, with a wish, with your mirror-image, with another person, etcetera.

Beliefs do not necessarily have to be the *Truth* – with a capital T. Chapter two gave you the story of someone who has not eaten Belgian endive for seventy years on the basis of one experience.
In the same way a lot of people believe certain 'truths' about themselves, about other people, or about society as a whole, on the basis of one personal experience or on the basis of one lesson they once learned from others.

Beliefs do not necessarily have to be the Truth – with a capital T

And you know painful experiences can make more of an impression than positive ones. It isn't strange that, as a rule, we drag along many beliefs which hinder us in our search for development and improvement.
Some people are even afraid of writing their goals down on paper. Or of discussing their goals with their partners or friends. It is the first step of saying goodbye to their current lives. Even if that current life is a life they are not really satisfied with, they do know exactly where they stand.

Useless beliefs overboard
Now how do we determine which beliefs we should get rid of and which are useful? It is hardly possible for us to research all things we believe in in a scientifically justified way, isn't? We should not do that. I suggest three practical steps.

First of all it is a big step if we realize that our beliefs don't form the *Truth*, but our *image* of the truth. It helps to regard your beliefs as the 'internal variety' of all kinds of external habits. Those are habits inside your mind, as you have habits in your speech or the way in which you clean up your closet.
I recently saw a TV program about the picture Americans have of the Netherlands. A man who was interviewed in the street maintained that the Netherlands was the capital of Denmark. As a rule, an American can easily get away with such a belief. But if you intend to go on vacation to the Netherlands, it is important to check your image of this reality beforehand.

Secondly, ask yourself the question whether your belief is really *right*. Most beliefs are *generalizations* which we form on the basis of one or a few experiences we have had or which we have shared with others.
Are you certain your belief is true always and everywhere? Can you really think of no exceptions?
And what actually is the source of your belief? What is the cause of you thinking the way you think? What is the tangible evidence for this? Can you give an example?
Just suppose: you are convinced that you should not start anything new without having looked at all the risks in advance. Does this mean you should never ever do anything before you have had a look at all ins and outs? Do you really believe that?
And what do you base that on? How many bad experiences have you gained before you came to this conclusion? One-hundred? Fifty? Twenty-five? Or maybe fewer?

Thirdly, ask yourself the question whether your belief is really *useful*. Suppose you continue acting in accordance with your current self-defeating belief, what would that bring you in the end? What is its final consequence?
Suppose you persist in the belief that you should not start anything

new before knowing all the risks. What would that mean then? Would not that boil down to you never starting anything new ever again? For you can never be completely sure whether you have really listed all possible pitfalls related to a particular intention.
And if that is the final consequence of your belief, how useful is that belief to you?

Dream, Dare, Do...

- Many people stay inside their NO area too long. They do see problems, pitfalls and threats, but can't take the step towards possible solutions.
- The YES area is the basis for development and growth. It is about us becoming more like the persons we are at our best moments.
- Many people are bothered by self-defeating beliefs. Ask yourself critically whether your beliefs about yourself and your plans are really true and are really useful.

'The night before I resigned we had been talking for hours'

After eight years of working in the financial sector, **Mary (33)** decided to resign and study obstetrics. In fact, she had wanted to go to medical school from an early age, but due to the lottery system in her country she failed to get a place in medical school: twice for medicine studies and once for obstetrics.
She decided to do something completely different and studied finance. But something kept nagging and she kept thinking every now and again, 'shouldn't I ...?' But there were always too many obstacles and she told herself to stop whining.

The change came when Mary got ill no less than seven times in the year after her first child was born. 'I wondered: what does my body actually want to tell me? It finally clicked when I read an article on happiness before I went to sleep. I realized I just had to study obstetrics anyway. I should stop thinking about the impossibilities, but try and find out what the possibilities are.
I immediately went to my computer and started searching the internet for information.'
Her search almost immediately gave her a comparable story about somebody who started studying again later in life. That strengthened Mary's belief that it can be done!

She tried to balance her feeling and reason for a full year to make sure she was making the right decision.
'In my heart I knew I really wanted to do this, but I wanted to be sure I would not make the wrong decision. Therefore, I talked to a lot of people who work as obstetricians and went to open days.'
Letting others know about her decision was a difficult step. 'I first kept it to myself for three weeks and only then told my husband. I only dared to tell my family and friends after five months. I was so afraid of the reactions. It was a very private thing and I felt very vulnerable about it. I wanted it so badly for myself, but still also wanted the support of others. I needed and need that so much.'

'Another thing that held me back was the notion of knowing the present but not the future. I was surprised that I stuck to that security so much.

Others often pointed out to me that I should have faith in a positive outcome. That turned out to be an essential aspect to me.'

I was surprised that I stuck to that security so much

In addition to the emotional side there were all kinds of practical matters which needed to be taken care of. Matters like finances and child care. That was difficult as well and cost time. When she finally received the letter of acceptance from the institute she knew that she couldn't back out anymore and really had to persevere.

'The night before I had to quit my job, we talked for hours. I still thought it was scary and all kinds of doom scenarios crossed my mind. I wanted my husband Raymond to support me all the way and fully realize what we were up against. His support was of vital importance to me. If you do something as radical as this, you are in it together. I still was not completely certain when I went to bed. The next morning before he left for work he said: "Just do it".'

Now all traces of doubt have disappeared. 'It is such a beautiful and inspiring job . I have found my niche. Even if it is difficult to combine everything. And of course I have my bad patches when it is very busy. But apart from that I strongly belief that I made the right choice. In four years I will be 37; I will have finished my studies and will be able to work another thirty years in a wonderful job.'

Dream, Dare, Do...

- Use your reason as well as your feeling when making choices. 'Choosing sensibly' against your feeling does not work. Making insensible choices in which you follow your heart does not work either.
- Do not think in obstacles but in possibilities. What do you really want and which steps are necessary to achieve this? Find out as much as possible: how did other people deal with this?
- Involve your loved ones actively in important choices, even if you don't look forward to this. You need their support later to be able to persevere.

6 Dream: and now for real...

- ***Why it is so important to translate your dreams into behavior***
- ***What is M.A.P. behavior and how do you formulate it?***
- ***What this effort brings you immediately***

A friend of mine coaches juvenile delinquents who have to get back to a paid job from a social security situation. Some time ago we discussed what his working days look like.

'Do you spend a lot of time on communicative skills and those sorts of things?', I asked.
'I would like to,' he said. 'But before I can do that, they first have to do a few other things.'
'You mean they first need to learn how to do the job. The craft side of it.'
'Yes, that as well. But usually I start with even more basic things.'
'Ok. I understand. You mean they first need to develop some self-confidence again or so,' I guessed.
'No,' he said. 'It is even more basic than you think. I can only teach them something when they *are* actually *there*. And that remains to be seen each and every morning. Especially when you have just started a new group. Quite a few of these guys don't take the notion of time seriously. Others call in sick at the slightest excuse. Others yet again don't feel like showing up at all. So usually I start the morning by visiting a few homes and getting the gentlemen out of their beds. And

only after they have learned after a while that they need to be there at eight o'clock each day, can we try to take a step further in other areas.'

Translation into behavior

Many people like dreaming about desirable end results. We read about somebody who started a *bed & breakfast* in the south of France and think: that is what I would like to do as well. We see somebody on TV in a beautiful home with a nice partner and nice kids. We hear this new singer who has become a big hit on the radio the last few months.

In most cases we only see that part of the story which has been achieved or realized after a lot of ups and downs. But the really unsuccessful sketches of an artist don't end up in a museum; they are thrown away! We don't hear about the doubts and fears of an actress who gets onto the stage for the very first time, unless it is later in an interview when she is already very successful.

In most cases we only see that part of the story which has been achieved or realized after a lot of ups and downs

If we want to realize something, want to change or improve something in our lives, we will have to look into the stories *behind* the success. We have to know which things you need to *do* to achieve the result. Which beliefs and actions take you to the place you want be?

Sometimes single shifts in our thoughts and single actions are involved, such as quitting a job which has made you miserable for a long time, for instance.

In most cases we don't reach our objectives by doing one thing. The question is usually which habitual thoughts and actions we need to make our own to really improve the quality of our lives in the long run.

For, also if we have quit this terrible job, the question definitely will arise: and now what? What are we going to do to spend the rest of our lives in a meaningful way?

Specify your dreams

There are three ways to specify your dreams. These three techniques help you to translate the direction you find important into behavior.

I advise you to use all three ways and first list a number of possible, concrete behavioral intentions. Only after you have done that, will you chose one or a few which you would like to start with.

1. Analyze your own successes from the past: go back to your YES area again and visualize as clearly as possible the moments which have inspired you to set your goals. What did you *do* at those moments? What did you *think*? And, very important, what did you *feel* then? Try to determine as accurately as possible which elements contributed to creating your best moments.

2. Ask advice from experts: imitate, read books, learn from others. My wife had not played tennis for years and recently started again. She plays with people who are fairly experienced. The other day I asked her whether she didn't dislike always being slaughtered during her tennis nights. 'Dislike? When I play with people who play worse than me I don't learn anything, do I? By playing with those people I improve each time!'

3. Reason and combine: your own success moments from the past and the things other people do are an important input for determining your behavioral intentions. But it may not be possible to repeat this exactly the same way in the here and now. Therefore you should try to choose behavior of which you are sure it suits you on the basis of the information you have gathered for this purpose.

M.A.P. behavior

Once you have made an inventory of a number of possible behavioral intentions it is a matter of choosing those behaviors which are *effective* and *feasible*. Behavior is only effective when you are sure it contributes to the goal you are trying to achieve. And behavior gets more feasible when you know that you are good at it and when you also receive appreciation from other people.

Make a list of possible intentions and give them a score on the basis of these two characteristics. The intentions which score highest on effectiveness and feasibility will have to be taken one step further. Try to translate them into Measurable, Active and Personal behavior.

Formulate your intentions in a M.A.P. way

- *Measurable*: how do you measure objectively and without discussion whether you have or have not brought your intentions into practice? How would an outsider measure what you do?
- *Active*: make clear what you *are* going to do. Which thoughts *are* you going to have? Which actions *are* you going to take?
- *Personal*: make clear what *you* are going to do! Of course others need to change all kinds of things in their lives as well, but you can't control that. They will have to do that *themselves*.

So do **not** get stuck in:

- *Vague* general intentions like: I will do my best more. When using terms like 'more' you never know afterwards whether a change succeeded or not!
- Making lists of things you do *not* want to do anymore, like: I want to stop complaining. It is impossible to actively *not* think about something. If I ask you *not* to consciously think of Brad Pitt for ten seconds with your eyes closed... who do you see in your mind's eye?
- Indicating what *others* need to change. For example: we need to improve our relationship. Who are 'we'? Wouldn't you rather start with *yourself*?

If I ask you not to consciously think of Brad Pitt who do you see?

What helps you to formulate your behavior in a measurable, active and personal way is to daydream goal-oriented. Make up a new film in your mind in which you try out your intended behavior. Try out a few intentions in your mind actively. Look closely at *what* you are doing during your daydreams. Visualize everything as clearly as possible. Then write it down.

After you have written down your intentions check whether you have used words like: *somewhat, a bit, improve, more, we, better, people,* etcetera. By definition these words are too vague.

Keep it simple!

During workshops that I give on self-management and change, formulating concrete behavior usually is the most difficult and at the same time the most valuable part. People, myself included, find it difficult to translate their goals into measurable, active, personal behavior.

A few mistakes which are often made:
- Getting stuck in abstract, vague terms. Although goals have been formulated, nobody knows exactly what has to be done to work into the direction of these goals.
- Goals are formulated in one area, but are opposed to goals which are set in other areas. An enormous boost of your career is difficult to combine with making more time for your loved ones. The word *individual* literally means *undividable*. Living one life is hard enough.
- Setting over-ambitious goals. Of course you can intend to do things which have never been done by anyone else before. Raising three kids, having a fulltime job next to that, paying enough attention to your partner and maintaining an extensive circle of friends. Well… I think the message is clear.

Something I have had to learn from personal experience: choose behavior which best suits you natural rhythm. Do not intend to do things which are too complex. Like: studying at 11.30 a.m. on Tuesdays; on Wednesdays at 8 p.m. to the sports club; and on Friday afternoons – every fortnight – helping my elderly neighbor. You understand that I am exaggerating, but many people make these kinds of complicated plans. Don't do that!

You'd better keep it simple. A few examples:
- Each morning before 11 a.m. I exercise at least ten minutes.
- Each night I make a note in my diary of the things which went well today, and which I want to do more of.
- Five minutes before I get home to my loved one, I ask myself how I want to enter the house, miserable and stressed, or happy and relaxed. I then have five more minutes to adjust my behavior.
- Each day I start by making a work plan in which I start with the rotten tasks and finish with the nicest things. I delete matters which, on second thoughts, are not important. If necessary, I call or e-mail people to tell them that I unfortunately will not manage to do these tasks.

Many people make complicated plans. Don't do that!

- Each lunch break I join different colleagues in the canteen in order to extend my network.
- At the start of each conversation I ask two questions at least before I start talking myself.

The staircase: start with something you are able to do
A picture which may help you is the following. Visualize a staircase. At the top of the staircase you will see the final result of what you want to achieve. All the stairs form the steps you will have to take – from bottom to top – on your way to your final goal.

At the top of the staircase you will find the final result.
The stairs are the steps on your way to your goal.

Now don't start at the bottom of the stairs as usual, but at the top. That is the way to reason backwards from your goal to the behavior which is necessary for reaching it.
Start at the top of the staircase and go down one step. What is behavior that is directly related to your goal? Is it something you already do or are able to do?
If not, go down another step and ask yourself the question again whether it is behavior you already display or are able to display.

Repeat this just as long as you have reached an action of which you are sure: I can do this. It is no use wanting to start behavior which is a step too high for you. That will only lead to more frustration and stress. Those are exactly the two things which are in the way of changes.

As an example: suppose you want to turn your career around. Another job, another area, maybe a completely new direction.

- At the top of the staircase is the result: a new job which does offer what you are looking for.
- The step before: applying for that job.
- The step before that: know which jobs really suit you.
- The step before that could be: trying out different jobs, for example through friends or through a temporary employment agency. Or do a series of sessions with a career coach.

Another example: you may want to become more assertive. Saying 'no' more often to things which make you unhappy.

- At the top of the staircase is your new, more assertive, more aware self.
- The step before is: always say 'no' to things which really do not suit you, or fit your diary, to everyone.
- The step before that is: say 'no' every once in a while to things which do not fit your diary, to everyone.
- Etcetera, etcetera, until the lowest step: to practice, tomorrow I will say 'no' to somebody I have arranged this with in advance.

If you say: 'Yes, but that's not difficult. I can do that.', you know you are on the right track.

If you say: 'Yes*, but that's not difficult. I can do that.*', you know you are on the right track.
If you say: *'Even the first step is too high!'* you just put smaller stairs in front of the first step.
In our example this could be asking somebody to first help you make your plans. Or practicing situations at home for a week in front of the mirror in which you say 'no' to an imaginary person.

'Right in one go' does not exist
If you see me jogging now you wouldn't know how badly I began. Armed with MP3 player, heart rate monitor and tight ventilating jog-

ging clothes, I regularly jog laps of eight miles or more. But when I started jogging a few years ago I did almost everything wrong that you can do wrong. I wore the wrong clothes and shoes. The distances were too short. And I ran much too slowly.
Only when I discussed my progress with an expert did I find out that I would achieve much better results if I adjusted a few simple things. Step by step I learned which method of training suits me best.

Even if you have thoroughly thought about the changes or improvements you want, eventually everything remains an experiment. By looking at your attempt to change like that you also make it less difficult. Whether you want to lose weight, want a new job, are looking for a partner or start exercising. The first attempts will always be clumsier than the things you do when you have more experience.

You may compare it to playing a game of darts. Nobody hits the bull's eye at the first throw. Usually you throw the first dart just to determine how far you are off center. So make sure you have enough darts. And start experimenting as soon as possible. Don't wait until you have read this book to begin (I suspect some people to read one self-help book after another so as just not to really have to do something). Try things out while you are still reading this book.

Chose behavior which you think could help you and check meticulously whether it works. Often it is useful to determine in advance a period for evaluation. For example: *if I do not see any improvement within two months I will consult an expert and adjust my approach.*

The focus effect

When you know what you want and what you are going to do a remarkable effect will come into force immediately. From the very first day you will notice all kinds of opportunities in your daily life to give shape to your intention. That isn't magic. Those opportunities have always been there. But until you know what you *want* and what you are going to *do* for it, you simply don't register them.

Our scope of attention is limited and is directed by our brain to matters which are of *importance* to us. By describing goals and behaviors in detail and making them important, our brain automatically focuses on things related to that.

When some time ago I promised to give a training in German for the first time, suddenly some of my friends from the south of the Netherlands turned out to master this language. Before that I had never wondered about this. And a lecturer with whom I worked appeared to be a German-speaking Swiss by birth. Of course I had noticed that he had a strange family name and he spoke with an accent. But until that time I had not paid any attention to it. These people helped me to bring my German to an acceptable level in two weeks.

Until you know what you want and what you are going to do for it, you simply don't register the opportunities

It is sometimes said that *you become what you regularly think of*. That is a bold statement. But there is some truth in it.
Positive and negative beliefs tend to reinforce themselves. This is logical. If you have a positive view of the world, you will see more possibilities for positive activities and have more positive experiences – at least in your perception. If you have a negative view of the world it works exactly the other way around.

Dream, Dare, Do...

- Dreams can only come true if you translate them into concrete behavior, that is measurable, active and personal (M.A.P.).
- It is important to always start with behavior which you know you can do. You can see changing as climbing stairs. Start with the step which you can reach.
- When you formulate your goals and related behavior concretely you will see more opportunities. These opportunities are always there, but you will only see them when they mean something to you.

'I thought: I will never finish my studies'

Irene was 23 and studied anthropology when she got pregnant. For some time after that she combined motherhood, her studies, working in a restaurant and at an office. But she never got around to finishing her studies.
Meanwhile the work at the office turned into a serious job. She had reached the age of thirty, was a mother of two, and pregnant with her third child.
Then she thought: 'I am just going to work; finishing my studies will never happen.'

'That is how it went for a few years. And I kept thinking: I have a job, I don't need to finish my studies anymore. With this I appeased my conscience as it were.
But in the mean time others kept asking what kind of education I had followed and then I had to tell them I had not finished it. That felt horrible'
The problem became bigger and bigger for Irene. 'I kidded myself that I could easily do it, but just had not. Meanwhile I became less secure and wondered whether I would indeed be able to do it.
I was very susceptible to the questions and remarks from others. There are quite a few people who didn't finish their studies and think this is ok. But to me it was not ok.'

Therefore Irene resumed her studies ten years after she had more or less stopped, and not half-heartedly, but with a clear plan and a deadline. 'Before my thirty-fifth birthday, which would be in two years, I wanted to be finished. I had made a very strict schedule. First I would follow a few lectures to get used to the system again. And I had decided to take some time off work when I had to write my thesis.'

Before my thirty-fifth birthday, in two years, I wanted to be finished

Her supervisor at university proved to be an important motivator. 'When I asked him: "Do you think I will be able to do it?", his reaction was: "Of course you can!" I thought "If he says so it must be true!"
That gave me a strange kind of motivation. But it worked. I wanted to prove myself to him as well.'
To be able to combine work, study and family she made clear arrange-

ments. She had asked her husband to help her and spend more time on taking care of the children temporarily. With her employer she arranged to work four hours less per week, which allowed her to follow lectures.
'As I didn't have much time, I used it efficiently. I appreciated the time I did have much more. For my thesis I took a three-month leave. This was during the summer vacation.
My husband and kids spent this time in a holiday park and I was home alone. Every now and again I felt really sad. But fortunately I am rather disciplined, and when I decide to do something, I really do it.'

In the end, writing the thesis was the most difficult thing. 'At the beginning I hated it. I had no idea how I should finish. Little by little I found out that I knew how to do it, and could do it, and that was a wonderful experience.
I persevered because I wanted it to be good. And yet in the final phase I was afraid I had failed completely. I remained insecure about the result.
I was very proud of course when I eventually scored a very high grade.
Looking back it has certainly been worth it!'

Dream, Dare, Do...

- If you know that it will be difficult to carry something through, prepare especially well. Avoid too much distraction and make sure you can really focus on the change you strive for.
- Many possible complications in a process of change can be indicated in advance. This means you can also think of a solution in advance.
- Find people who believe in you and who want to help you with important changes. That is very motivating.

7 Dare: knowing your moments of crisis in advance

- ***What we can learn from Lance Armstrong***
- ***How do you determine your moments of crisis in advance?***
- ***How stress and exhaustion lead to relapse***

I am not a real cycling aficionado. But it very much fascinates me how Lance Armstrong managed to win the Tour de France more times than all riders before him. In his book *Every second counts* he shares some of his secrets with the readers.
Armstrong describes how he is under pressure after his first victory in 1999 to perform again. In order to prepare he explores all heavy stages of the Tour in the spring of 2000. On a cold day on which it is raining and snowing at the same time he does the Hautacam. This is a steep mountain near the town of Lourdes.

Armstrong rides the heavy climb in about an hour, but when he gets to the top he isn't satisfied. He feels he hasn't divided his energy well. 'We need to go back to do it once again,' he says to his team leader. In half an hour Armstrong descends again to the foot of the mountain and starts again with the same climb. When he arrives at the top for the second time – soaked with rain and snow – he feels he controls the mountain.

Some months later the Hautacam is the first mountain stage in the Tour of 2000. And when Armstrong wakes up that morning, the weather turns out to be 'perfect'. It is icy-cold and it is raining. The other riders clearly dread a day full of sweat and pain. But Armstrong smiles. Those are exactly the circumstances he prepared for. And, moreover, he only has to go to the top *once* this day.

When they approach the mountain the cyclists have already been on their bikes for four hours. Together with some other cyclists Armstrong starts the climb. At a steep part he knows well he attacks and leaves them behind apparently without any effort.
Later he says about this: 'I had not only trained my legs for this jump up the Hautacam but also my attitude.' In the end Armstrong takes the lead by minutes on his most important competitors during this ascent. That day he wins the yellow jersey and doesn't let go of it for the rest of the Tour.

Why people relapse
Lance Armstrong's story contains a few clear lessons for everyone who wants to give a good performance. Also for ordinary people like you and me.
The first lesson for me is that each achievement knows its moments of truth. The moments which really count. In the Tour of 2000 this was the climb of the Hautacam, amongst other things.
The second lesson is that winning doesn't come automatically. Armstrong doesn't rely on his talent and strength blindly. He explores the most difficult stages of the Tour in advance and if necessary he even practices a climb twice consecutively.
And the third lesson is that such a preparation has a double effect. You are not only physically better capable of winning the stage, but you are also mentally stronger than the rest. Not only your skill, but also your spirit gets a boost.

At the same time you also understand better why so many people do not succeed.

- They do not explore the most difficult part of their development or change process. Moments of crises will strike unexpectedly. And/or:
- They rely a bit too much on making it even if things get rough on the way. They do not realize that moments of crisis almost always lead to (old) automatic behavior. And/or:

- They have not got the skills and courage to persevere at difficult moments *simply because* they have not prepared well enough.

Not only your skill, but also your spirit gets a boost

The above conclusions may sound a bit harsh. But if I am honest I know that my own attempts to change went wrong for the same reasons.
The times I relapsed into old, ineffective habits while I had sometimes only just started, often full of optimism, were *always* caused by ending up in a difficult situation for which I had not prepared.

- I quit smoking years ago. But in all failed attempts to quit in the past I relapsed in times of extreme stress.
- For a few years I have exercised regularly. But all attempts to exercise more before that failed during times of large work related stress and 'no time' for half an hour of sports a week.

In chapter 1 I already stated that eventually more than eighty percent of all people who start a change turn out to relapse into old habits within two years. And relapsing doesn't take place on just any day of the week, just because they feel like it, but at moments of crisis, of which almost all of them say afterwards: *'I should've known! If only I had persevered then, things would've been very different now.'*

Moments of truth

In the movie *Sliding Doors* Gwyneth Paltrow is Helen. Helen is a young working woman who is fired and goes home after that. On her way home she only just catches the metro train. The sliding doors close right behind her. As she gets home early she discovers her boyfriend cheats on her with his ex-girlfriend. She leaves this unfaithful loser and becomes happy with another man who is much nicer and – like her – a Monty Python fan.
The nice touch to this film is that a *second* story starts simultaneously. The story about what it would have been like when the sliding doors had closed just a little sooner and Helen had missed the metro. In that story she is robbed at the empty metro platform and comes home after being treated in hospital. Then her boyfriend is taking a shower and his ex-girlfriend has already left.
Although he doesn't do much else than cheating on Helen, he claims

he is writing a book. In order to help him in his strive for becoming an author Helen takes two jobs and becomes rather unhappy.
Well. Rent the DVD and have a fascinating evening.

What everyone with a bit of life experience knows, and what the film shows in a nice way, is that some moments play a crucial role in your life. These are the moments in which you sometimes make active choices (but sometimes also react passively to the things which happen to you) because of which the further course of your life's history can be changed completely.
The annoying thing is that we often only realize afterwards that we have experienced such a moment.

Imagine what it would mean if we could actively prepare for such moments of truth.
Naturally, in our daily lives it is impossible to plan and manage everything. But the nice thing about planned changes and personal development, which this book is about, is that you can often easily point out these moments of truth in advance.
If you work on an important change in your life, it is logical to spend time and energy on this.

The first step is the hardest
In this chapter we try to determine which situations, in which you are likely to relapse into old behavior, you may encounter during your change process. In the next chapter you will be given a few powerful techniques which will help you to persevere nevertheless.

It may surprise you, or not, but a lot of people who want to change relapse immediately at the start.
Leaving behind old behavior and doing new things especially at the beginning leads to feelings of insecurity. Other people will also have to get used to your new behavior. And it will usually take a long time before your results are apparent to you.
As old behavior usually *does* lead to a good feeling the chance that you relapse at the start is very large.

Some time ago I contributed to a training session for employees of garages. These people had finally discovered what the rest of the

world already knew: they were not customer-friendly enough. Especially the chief-mechanics who had to speak to customers scored disappointingly low in all research.
In several workshops these employees (mainly men aged between forty and fifty) discussed about what they could do to improve. For example, they wanted to welcome the customer within ten seconds of arrival and ask how they could help him or her.

My colleagues will think: just listen to that slimeball!

Subsequently they were asked which problems they were likely to encounter. First they were not very eager to say something about this as they were after all amongst colleagues. But in the end one of them took up courage to say something. *'When we talk to our customers like that for the first time next Monday I am afraid my colleagues will listen in behind the door. I am afraid I will be in a cold sweat and that they all think: just listen to that slimeball!'*

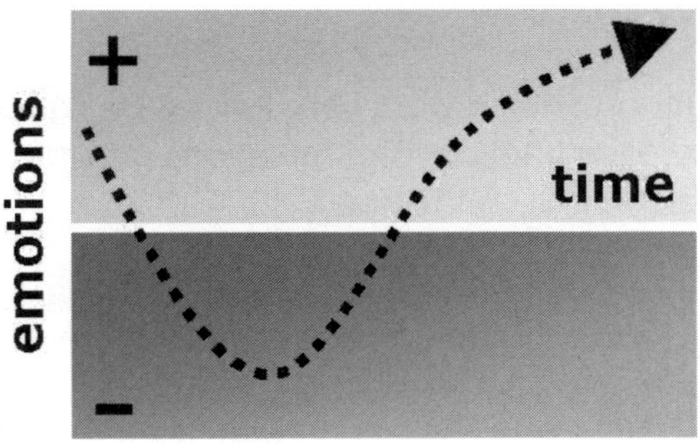

At the beginning of our change process we often feel insecure and frustrated…

Typical relapse situations
The crisis situations at the beginning of our change process and the moments of stress which occur later on have one thing in common. They contain all kinds of stimuli which strongly reactivate our old behavior which we want to overcome.

While you are trying to move your life consciously and planned into another direction, these kinds of situations cause some of the buttons on our MP3 player to be pushed hard to replay the old hit song.

A few examples:

- From now on you would like to be friendlier and more patient towards your partner. But when you do something stupid, you will get lectured at – of course completely unjustly as far as you are concerned.
- From now on you would like to show more understanding for people around you and control your anger. But on your bike you are cut off by a young motorist in a twenty-year old car with sports exhaust.
- You would like to live a healthier life and not eat fast food anymore. But this week your youngest has a party and the table is full of cake, muffins, chocolate and French fries.
- You started to work one day a week less, but now your company gets a large order and everyone is expected to help out. They also appeal to you for assistance.

I've been in all four situations. And I have learned by experience that you can only succeed in bringing your intentions into practice if you are prepared for these kinds of situations.

The beautiful thing is that we are equipped with a mechanism to spot these situations in advance. These are the situations which make us nervous or even scare us in advance.

It is healthy to be afraid every now and again. If there were nothing we are afraid of we would not live a long life. And fear can also help you to point out those situations that are crucial. Those situations in which you have to show courage. Those situations in which you literally have to conquer your fears.

Unexpected crisis situations

It is difficult to make a start. We all know this to be true. And by listening to our fears we can indicate a few other 'moments of truth' beforehand.

But, you might think, *I can't possibly foresee all ordeals in advance.* Will you ever manage to be prepared for everything and anything that can go wrong? On a bad day a completely unexpected crisis will occur and you will still give in!

This is true, but then again it is not. It is true there will be unexpected crisis situations. But this doesn't necessarily have to mean that you will fall down and relapse into the old habits you want to get rid of.

It is in fact very well possible to protect yourself against unexpected incidents and situations. You know one thing for sure: unexpected things are bound to occur. And it could happen that all kinds of crises which you have thought of in advance will be much more difficult than you expected.
Therefore I advise you to choose a remedy in any case from the next chapter. These remedies are especially meant for *unexpected crisis situations or expected crisis situations which turn out to be unexpectedly complicated.*
These can be like a sort of First-Aid kit in your mind. Whenever unexpectedly an accident happens you are ready to deal with it.

Stress and exhaustion
Sometimes people say they perform best under high pressure. I recognize that. I may be able to write a good column or a nice article without a deadline, but I can do much better *with* a deadline.
On the other hand it is true that too much pressure will undermine our performances. If I have to write a column in a quarter of an hour, while this usually takes an hour at least, I have a problem.
Situations which lead to high pressure, which cause stress, usually cause us to forget our intentions, cause us to be less creative in looking for new options and so cause us to relapse into old habits. Of course these are usually those habits we were trying to get rid of.

Moreover, stress appears to become stronger automatically. Remember how your latest row developed. You probably found yourself in a situation in which you were under a lot of pressure. You had to rush for an appointment. Or somebody said something which bothered you. Or both. That works even better!
This caused the production of stress hormones in your body which made you say something nasty in return. And that made the situa-

Subsequently, you had a flaming row and asked yourself afterwards why these things have to go like this

tion even tenser, which caused a multiplication of your (and the other person's) stress hormones.
And, subsequently, you had a flaming row. At a certain moment you didn't even realize what you said anymore and asked yourself afterwards why these things have to go like this. (Of course this little story gives you the answer to your question.)

Especially situations in which we feel pressured, or situations in which we feel very tired, are exhausted after a day of hard work, are typically situations in which we tend to relapse. In those situations we don't enjoy our good intentions anymore and only feel the pain that changing involves.

Anticipation really helps

The German researcher Peter Gollwitzer has, for many years, researched the effects of anticipation on moments of crisis. It appeared that making simple plans in advance to persevere in problem situations increases our chance of success dramatically.

An example from his research: just before the Christmas break Gollwitzer asked his students to hand in a report 48 hours after Christmas Eve on how they spent this evening. He told them he researched the way students in Germany spend their spare time.

The first group was only given this assignment. Gollwitzer probably wished them good luck and 'Fröhliche Weihnachten' and sent them off.
The other group of students was given the same assignment, but they were also asked to write down in advance when and where they would write their reports. Gollwitzer thought that Christmas time normally isn't the best time to write reports. Having a good time with friends, getting together with your family and other outings make it very difficult to get some work done as well during this time.

The results were remarkable. Of the group of students who had not thought about how they were going to schedule writing this report in this difficult time 33% sent in the report before the deadline.

Of the group of students who had consciously scheduled to finish the report, 75% sent the report to Gollwitzer before the deadline.

Other researches done by Gollwitzer and his assistants show similar results. Preparing for difficult moments increases the chance of a successful execution of your intentions by a factor of three to four! The next chapter is entirely dedicated to this topic.

Dream, Dare, Do...

- People do not relapse into old behavior 'just like that'. It happens at moments of crisis which they have often foreseen well in advance.
- Stress and exhaustion are factors which cause relapse into old, ineffective habits. This often happens at the beginning of a change.
- Actively anticipating moments of crisis turns out to be very effective. The chance of perseverance increases by a factor of three to four.

'I had completely lost control of my daily agenda'

Two years ago **Harold (31)** became co-owner of a consultancy after having worked as a self-employed consultant for years. 'The first few months were very difficult for me. I managed almost two full companies next to each other because former clients still called me. I also felt I was very young to be doing what I was doing. I knew people who worked in my new company looked at me as their example and I felt I just couldn't be that. '

'I also had the feeling I was controlled by my daily agenda. I felt I was no longer in control. At the beginning I could still put things in the right perspective, but at a certain moment the pressure became too large. In my private life all kinds of things were happening as well and I couldn't relax anywhere. I felt stressed and rather hopeless.'

Harold talked over his problem during a jogging session with one of his friends.
'At a certain moment he asked me whether I could think back to something I succeeded in, something which I considered a success. While we were talking I came up with the fact that I had stopped smoking. I smoked two packages a day, was heavily addicted and stopped with the help of a course. That was a difficult battle.
This made me realize that a process of change is a battle and doesn't happen overnight. That was really the moment that I realized I could change and just had to do it.'

I felt stressed and rather hopeless

'At my work I started making arrangements to get more control. The most important arrangement is that my organizer stays empty before half past nine. In this way I can first have a look at my schedule for that day, read my e-mails and make urgent telephone calls. Otherwise these kinds of things will be on your mind all day. Closing the day in a calm way is important as well. I noticed immediately that you really have to stick to these arrangements for yourself, but also for others. Otherwise you will easily fall back into your old ways. Next to that I started "fighting" as well. When I saw things were not working, I immediately looked for a solution. The talks during my jogging sessions have helped me tremendously. I had gotten an enormous drive and new energy. I saw that it worked and that motivated me to continue.'

The most difficult moment was during the summer. 'I just returned from my vacation and lost control completely for weeks. I had a lot of extra work, all kinds of meetings and noticed that my position was changing. People regarded me more and more as a co-owner. I had lost control of my daily agenda again and had the feeling I wasn't able to get down to doing anything. That was a scary feeling.
I started talking to two people I had chosen consciously and focused again on the moment I quit smoking. I reminded myself of how horrible that time was and how large the temptation was to start smoking again. But also how happy I was that I persevered.
And I started sticking to my own arrangements again consciously. The most important rule remains: Start the day calmly and finish the day calmly.'

'Three weeks ago it was very hectic again and I noticed that I didn't start to panic. I just thought: "Oh well, it's just a hectic week, so what?" Whenever it gets too much now, I consciously try and find somebody to talk to.
In fact, I have been able to change a lot in a short period. I've learned a lot and it gives me a real thrill that it worked out successfully!'

Dream, Dare, Do...

- Create enough space and overview when you want to change things. Stress and exhaustion can easily cause you to relapse into old, ineffective habits.
- Remind yourself of your success moments. Moments in which you put up a good performance which you still feel proud of.
- Search actively for people with whom you can talk. Discuss the problems and possible solutions. Often you develop new insights on the basis of these talks.

8 Dare: controlling difficult moments

- ***Techniques which help at difficult moments***
- ***The importance of calling in assistance***
- ***No time for changing? A few practical tips!***

Last year visitors to my website *www.tiggelaar.com* could do a change test. In this test – which you can find in the back of this book – questions were asked about the way they deal with changes. Whether they translate their wishes into behavior beforehand, whether they anticipate problematic situations, etcetera. On the basis of their answers they were assessed as a good, mediocre or bad changer.
More than five thousand people took the test. What struck me was that the topic of this chapter was an important breaking point.

As it happens most people answered that they *were able* to point out difficult moments beforehand, but *were not able* to think of ways to persevere anyway. They did know where things would go wrong but didn't do anything with this knowledge.
Actually, this is a bit clumsy, isn't it? Scaring yourself with all kinds of crisis situations which will interfere with your change but not thinking about how you can continue nevertheless.
I suspect that many people do not even start a change process because of this. Contemplating crises beforehand will certainly cause them to lose courage.
Earlier on I said that each step in this book is also a test for your motivation. Although the techniques in this book are meant to make

changes run smoother and more effectively they will cost some effort in themselves as well.
First you will have to put some effort into reading and understanding them. And subsequently it will cost attention, energy and time to apply them in practice. I realize that for some people this is a difficult task.
The alternative is, however, that *you do what you always did, and get what you always got*. A bit of a cliché. But then, that's what clichés are: a simple truth.

Three techniques that work

Which techniques help us to persevere at the moments of crisis? How do we prevent ourselves from relapsing?

Many people think that you will get there if you have enough willpower. 'You have to really want it,' people will say. Sounds good, but in real crises this isn't true. These kinds of situations cause a lot of stress by definition. We are pressured by incidents and people in our direct environment. And under large stress our conscious control fails and we act on automatic pilot.
What may be the most annoying thing: if you try to gain a victory for your long-term interests on your short-term interests by using your willpower at these kinds of moments your stress will only increase. It is a downward spiral in which your old habits will eventually win.

Another type of advice you sometimes hear is: avoid situations in which you tend to relapse. Although this is more sensible, it isn't a long-term solution. As a former smoker you will one day have to face your friends who still smoke. As a former candy lover you will one day have to pass the bargains at the checkout at the supermarket.
But I admit: at the beginning it is sensible to avoid exactly those stimuli which cause relapses. It may be a good idea to start changes at moments in which you don't have much stress. For example in a longer vacation (beware: the first days of a vacation are very stressful for a lot of people). But do realize that you will have to confront harsh reality some day.

Under large stress our conscious control fails and we act on automatic pilot

What else is left?

You can control the situation by adding extra stimuli to your moments of crisis. Stimuli which help you to persevere in your intended behavior. You could say that we push a few other buttons on our MP3 player on purpose at the moments which are relevant. And we do this in the form of *reminders* (technique number one: stimuli preceding behavior) and *rewards* (technique number two: stimuli following behavior).
For example: you would like to say 'no' more often to certain requests at work. Remind yourself beforehand (for example, by writing it on your hand) and reward yourself afterwards when you have actually said 'no' (do something or say something to yourself which you really like).

Next to that we can train ourselves to actively start different behavior at difficult moments. This should be behavior which helps us to execute our intentions. This is called *countering* (technique number three).
A simple example of countering is taking a *time-out*. Instead of immediately reacting to other people's remarks you take a short break. By doing this you actively lead your attention into a different direction. After the first frustration or temptation has subsided somewhat it is much easier to stick to your intentions.

Technique number one: reminders to help you dare more
To remind yourself of important intentions at difficult moments anything is allowed. I will give you a few suggestions....

- Your organizer is a good place to remind yourself daily of the directions you have chosen and of your behavioral intentions. For years, I have used a card in my organizer on which I have written these things. Each week this card moves to the week we live in.
- Put stickers with reminders for yourself in places where you need them. For example on your refrigerator, on your computer, on your TV or in other places which tempt you to do things you don't want to do.
- Put a note in your wallet for the moment you end up in 'the unexpected situation'. On this note write your deepest personal reason for working on your change.

- Make a bracelet (or have one made) which reminds you of your objectives and your intentions.
- Imagine difficult moments as realistically as possible beforehand. Subsequently choose something inside these moments which you are going to use as a 'trigger' for your own intention: 'When *that* happens, when they do *that*, I will do what I have intended to do.'

In addition to this it is a good idea to make arrangements with people around you. Ask them to help you in your change process. If people who are dear to you are not informed of the change you want, you will make it very difficult on yourself.

If people who are dear to you are not informed of the change you want, you will make it very difficult on yourself

Other people with whom you are in touch a lot have a large influence on your behavior by definition. That influence can either be positive or negative. By making arrangements you can make this influence work in the right direction.

- Arrange with your partner to remind each other in difficult situation of a specific intention, for example with a certain signal.
- Arrange with colleagues to support each other in a certain change. For example by discussing it weekly during one of your lunches.

A few practical tips for the use of reminders:

- Use words or signals with an emotional meaning. Put your own name at the top of your reminder notes. You will definitely look at them more often.
- Vary your reminders regularly. If you are used to a certain reminder it doesn't work anymore and it is time for a different stimulus.

Technique number two: rewards to help you dare more

In the next chapter I will go into rewarding yourself more deeply and reinforcing behavior with these rewards. It is important to make it *extra attractive* for yourself to persevere in difficult situations.

Ward off the powerful short-term frustration of a crisis situation with a short-term reward which is twice to three times as big. The reward to continue should be so attractive that you would have to be a fool to let it go.

What could you have in mind? A few suggestions:

- Give yourself points for each day that you continue your new behavior and bonus points for continuing in difficult situations. When you get to one hundred points: take a day off, go to the shopping mall and buy new clothes. Or something else which you really like.
- Celebrate your perseverance immediately afterwards. Take the rest of the day off and reward yourself with a relaxed afternoon and evening. Buy a new book, take a long bath, watch a new DVD. In short, enjoy and tell yourself at least ten times how proud you are of yourself for having persevered.

Also when you reward the perseverance during crises it is worthwhile to call in assistance. Make arrangements with friends, colleagues or your partner.

- If you know it is going to be a tough day, arrange to have dinner that evening to celebrate your success.
- Arrange for your loved one to have a surprise for you at the moments you persevered. The element of surprise makes the reward even larger from your point of view.

Some people are somewhat frightened by lavish rewards. That is quite logical if you come from a culture, like I do, in which the cookie jar is closed after you have been offered one cookie.
Don't misunderstand me; I don't plead unbridled hedonism. Like: let it all hang out, let your hair down and do whatever you like. I am trying to make clear that you can't compete against the frustrating power of a crisis situation if you do not offer something stronger in exchange.

Technique number three: countering to help you dare more
Countering is defending yourself actively with your own behavior against the opposing stimuli of crisis situations. You actively prevent yourself from falling back into old habits which you want to get rid of. A number of suggestions which you can use in expected and unexpected problem situations are given below.

Talking: one of the most common forms of countering. Talk to yourself in difficult situations. Out loud or inside your head. During skiing, when I come to a slope which is in fact too steep for me, I control the fear and stress by talking to myself out loud while I go down the mountain.

It works exactly the same with crisis situations in a personal change process. Think of a number of things you can say to yourself in problem situations. Things like: *'You have prepared for this. This is it! When you persevere you are a hero. You know you can do it; do it!'*

In the same way you can fight fatalistic thoughts. When you get negative thoughts you say to yourself: *'STOP. Now!'* and then remind yourself of the top performance from your own past. A memory from the centre of your YES area.

Thinking: train yourself to think in images. I have trained myself to automatically conjure up an image in my mind of somebody who is much too fat every time I drive past a drive-through restaurant. This is very simple: take the restaurant logo in your mind and exchange it a few times with a frighteningly fat person. And then I mean really, really frightening! If you continue this for a minute or so the next time when you see the logo this picture automatically comes to mind.

Of course this is awfully childish! But it has helped me for a few years

Of course this is awfully childish! But it has helped me for a few years not to turn off at each drive-through restaurant and order a hamburger menu.

What also helps us is to view crisis situations in a distorted form on purpose. Actively look for the humor in a crisis. Or look at matters very clinically and distantly on purpose. In this way you prevent yourself from relapsing automatically into old behavior.

Train yourself in thinking in images

Moving: your posture has an immediate effect on how you feel. When you sit or stand more upright and when you laugh it immediately has a positive effect on your self-confidence. Why don't you try it?
When you move faster than you normally do, you give yourself a boost. On the other hand, when you move more slowly than you normally do, you calm down. By breathing more quickly you activate yourself, but by breathing more calmly you make yourself more passive.
During my seminars I often do some physical exercises with music. It is unbelievable what kind of effect this has on the participants' moods. The best advice I can give you is to experiment with your own posture, movement and breathing. Discover the effect it has on your thoughts and feelings. Train a few times when you know you will be facing a crisis situation.

Feeling: all of the above forms of countering have a direct effect on your feelings. A stimulus with which you can fundamentally influence your feelings is music. By playing my favorite music in my car before a seminar or a difficult meeting I get out with a good feeling.

Make sure that you always have some music with you in difficult times. You can give yourself a boost or calm yourself down with it.
You can also actively evoke feelings with images in your mind. It helps, for example, to imagine consciously how much you will regret letting the investment you have made so far slip through your fingers under the pressure of the situation or under the pressure of a few other people.
You just try it. Experiment with your emotional management. If you don't take control yourself, others will do it for you.

No time for a change!
One of the things which forms an obstacle for starting and continuing a change is a lack of time. A day only has 24 hours and there is so much to do. You could say that time management is a special form of countering. By planning your time better you create space for changes you find important.

The American author Stephen Covey recommends that we categorize everything we do into importance and urgency. The advantage is that you have already decided what is important to you in the preceding chapters!
Take your organizer or calendar and ask yourself: which things were mainly important and which were mainly urgent?

- How much time do you spend on matters which are not important and not urgent, like watching TV?
- How much time is spent on matters which are not important, but still urgent, like many interruptions by e-mail or phone calls?
- How much time do you spend on matters which are important and urgent? Important matters you in fact have left untouched too long?
- And how much time do you spend on matters which are important and not urgent? The things that are most useful to you in the long run?

Almost all people underestimate how busy they will be in a few weeks, now that their organizers still look empty

By analyzing critically how you spend your time you will discover possibilities for improvement. When you then fill out your organizer for the coming time you first plan time for matters which are important but *not yet* urgent. Like for example working on your change.

In addition to that it is sensible to reserve a fixed part of the day for urgent and important matters. The important e-mails, voicemails and telephone conversations. A fixed period will prevent you from reacting to these kinds of outside impulses all day long.
Almost all people *underestimate* how busy they will be in a few weeks, now that their organizers still look empty. That is why we are often overconfident when making promises to ourselves and others. So be fair and honest to yourself.

If any other important tasks remain plan them in accordance with the F.L.A.T. method: First Least Attractive Tasks.

- Make an overview of your tasks in the morning.
- Rank them from one to ten; one being the least attractive job and ten the most attractive job.
- Then start with the least attractive tasks.
- Each next task is a reward for the previous in this way.
- The day starts with an overview and ends with the most attractive task.

A three-step plan

During the first seminars I gave about self-management, I still asked people to answer fifteen questions related to their intended change in a workbook. For many participants this proved to be frustrating. They got stuck because they couldn't clearly formulate the answers or ran out of time.

Now I use easy worksheets with only a few main questions.

A simple worksheet with three essential steps. For more work material please check www.tiggelaar.com

In fact this is all there is. But of course you understand that posing these questions is a lot easier than answering them. Going through this process often goes with a lot of ups and downs.

It is sensible to write down your (preliminary) answers and look at them regularly. By writing your plans on paper you help yourself to think about them much more clearly and in a better way.

Dream, Dare, Do...

- Reminders help you to continue at difficult moments. You need to remind yourself powerfully of your intentions when it is needed most.
- Rewarding helps as well. Attack the short-term frustration of a crisis moment with a reward which is at least twice to three times as large.
- Countering is the third technique which is effective in moments of crisis. Talking actively, moving, thinking and feeling to defend yourself against relapsing into old habits.

'Since I started my own company there are difficult moments continuously'

Claudia (41) started her own company recently: Health-Gym. As a gym teacher she developed gym programs which you can do sitting down on a chair (for example in your car in a traffic jam) or lying in bed (for example in hospital) as physical training. She'd had the plan to start her own company for years. Experience and especially the support of others were necessary to finally really start.

'Twenty years ago I already rented my first little gym where I gave physical education classes. But then I still had a lot to learn. I only had my basic knowledge and little experience in teaching and little experience in life. Since then I have always been employed as a physical education teacher. I taught people in all kinds of age brackets and all types of schools.'

Eight years ago Claudia got pelvic instability which prevented her from being able to walk. 'Nothing helped and I started looking for a solution because I wanted to be cured. Then I found the exercises on which I have based my company. After four weeks I could do everything again.
Subsequently, I worked it out on the basis of that principle. I learned a lot and now know exactly why it works.
Last year I started to study sports massage and chair massage and that turned out to be the start of a network. Through this network I met a lot of people. One of those people started his own company from scratch. He supported me with practical matters and that encouraged me to persevere.'

Stimulating people are very important to Claudia. 'If somebody said "oh, why bother" I often put my own ideas and dreams aside quickly. I really need people who believe in me.
For me entrepreneurship is also about cooperation. It starts with an idea and after that you look for the experts who can help you with their know-how to realize this idea. People who listen, but who also ask critical questions. That makes me think again and makes me find new solutions. In this way new things cross your path again and again. The people around me are very precious to me. I thank them with a card or an

e-mail. Inform them of what I am working on. I value what they do and always return their attention.'

In practice it is not easy to persevere. 'There have been difficult moments continuously right from the start. Money is a problem. And there is also a lot of opposition from people in my surroundings. People who don't understand I want to start my own company and quit my job at a certain moment. Many people look at it this way. In my home I put up a lot of maxims and sayings to get me through these difficult moments. I look at them regularly and that helps.'

'Even if I am sometimes scared out of my wits, I do continue'

'I notice that you have to stick your neck out to be an entrepreneur. You run risks, put in money and you need to have deep-rooted trust in what you want to do and what you are capable of. This is very difficult and you don't always persist.
As I have already developed myself a lot I do have a better balance and have become more decisive. And, fortunately, every time I have a lousy experience nice experiences follow. There are people who believe in me. And then I think "Yes, I do have to continue".
Ups and downs remain. But I do have the feeling I will get there in the end. And even if I am sometimes scared out of my wits, I do continue.'

Dream, Dare, Do...

- Many people cherish certain dreams and ambitions for years. You will only get things going when you start a learning process. Simply by *doing* it.
- Find people around you who inspire and motivate you. Everybody needs inspiration and encouragement when they want to realize major changes.
- Realize that large changes will never be realized at once. It is a process of ups and downs and can sometimes take years.

9 Do: starting with ups and downs

- ***How children and adults learn***
- ***Measuring: easy tips to measure your behavior***
- ***Why you should reward behavior instead of rewarding results***

My daughter Emma still needs to learn to ride a bicycle. She has been riding it with training wheels for a long time, but she should learn to ride it properly soon. She wants it herself: without help, really riding a bike.
As I have helped my first two children learn to ride a bike I know how it works. But suppose I would like to do it differently this time.

I would, as an experiment, try out on Emma the approach which is generally used in education for youngsters and adults. I would place a projector and a screen in the living room, sit Emma down on a chair and subsequently give a presentation of half an hour on for example... 'the history of the bicycle'. I would start with the invention of the wheel. Explain that first there were only boneshaker bicycles which people rode by moving their feet on the floor. And I would probably end with a few stories about famous cyclists such as Eddie Merckx, Bernard Hinault, and Lance Armstrong.

After a short break I would continue for half an hour with the 'functioning of the organ of balance'. This would be part of the obligatory theory for five-year olds who want to learn to ride a bicycle.

After the full presentation I would remove the training wheels from her bike, put her on the saddle and wish her good luck: 'You now know how it works, so go ahead!'

Everybody knows it doesn't work like that. If you want to teach your children how to ride a bike, you will have to run next to them and encourage them. And 'balance' isn't a theory that should be taught but something you need to experience during the ride. You need to *feel* it in your handlebars.
Children learn by immediate feedback. They sense whether it goes well or badly. They hang to one side too much and feel they almost fall. Then they correct very quickly with the handlebars. That's how it works.

Feedback: measuring and rewarding behavior
The largest misconception about learning is that the learning process looks different once we have grown up, that we should learn in a 'more adult' way. On the basis of research as well as on the basis of my own personal experience I know that this thought is absolute nonsense.
The immediate experience determines whether we continue the behavior or not. Immediate pain causes us to cease new behavior at once, or in any case after a few attempts. Immediate pleasure causes us to continue. It sounds simple, and in fact it is very simple. Adults also need immediate feedback on their behavior.

When you want to lose weight, for example, to feel better, you know that the result you are trying to achieve in the end often is months away. That makes it very difficult to continue. You don't succeed on the basis of your original 'natural' motivation alone.
You will have to stimulate the *behavior* necessary to reach your goal 'artificially' until the first results are really visible. You will have to choose things or activities which are a motivator, a reward for goal-oriented behavior.

Some people do not understand why you have to reward *behavior* and not the results. But in fact this is very logical. Almost all changes which are worthwhile run the same course. The results follow in the long run while we have to invest from the very first day by means of our behavior.

Sometimes the only thing we can do is influence our own behavior while we can hardly or not at all influence the results. We do what is right but don't expect a lot of results immediately.

The results follow in the long run while we have to invest from the very first day by means of our behavior

Feedback consists of two elements: measuring and rewarding. You will have to measure your behavior and subsequently determine whether you have executed your intention right or not. Only when you have executed your intended behavior right, will you reward yourself. It is important that you are a bit strict on yourself and very consistent!

Measuring and rewarding can sometimes be done during or immediately after the behavior. Immediately after having been to the sports centre for one and a half hours you are entitled to relax with a good book or a good detective on TV.

Sometimes it is a bit more difficult to arrange feedback at the moment itself. It may help to take a fixed moment for this. You could, for example, reflect on the past day each night or each morning. Go through the day in your mind. Make a note of your 'score' on a list and reward yourself.

Measuring your own behavior

It may sound strange. Definitely if you still don't like the idea of keeping track of all kinds of things about yourself. But to many people just keeping track of things and measuring their own behavior turns out to be an important boost!

To make measuring effective and fun, I will give your three tips. Measure at least once a day, at a fixed time and on the basis of a simple list.

- *Measure once a day at least*: this is definitely essential during the first few weeks of a change process. Each moment you measure gives you the opportunity to work on your intention and stimulate yourself. You evaluate, look ahead and reward yourself in your mind or in a concrete way.
- *Fixed time*: choose a fixed time each day in which you spend a few

minutes on your change. For example immediately at breakfast, during lunch or before going to bed. If you make measuring too difficult for yourself, you will not succeed. Try to do this at a natural, relaxed moment.

- *Simple list*: draw up a list on which you can easily check or tick off whether you have succeeded in bringing your intention into practice. Make it as simple as possible. Then measuring becomes easier and much more fun. Make sure you always have the list within reach. Put it in your organizer, or take it with you in your wallet or in your bag.

Some people think measuring is childish. They think that adults can just do these kinds of things in their minds. Unfortunately this is a misconception. As our behavior is only controlled to a small extent by willpower and to a large extent by habits we generally forget these things too easily.

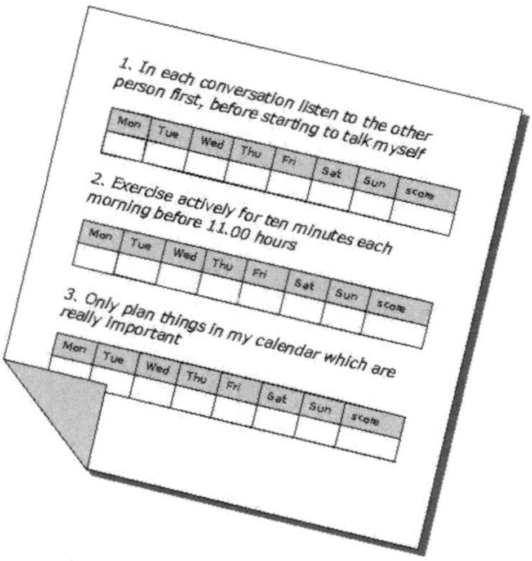

Keep your lists to measure your behavior clear and simple

Rewarding your own behavior
We have talked about rewarding behavior before. It is especially important to clearly link the reward in our minds to the behavior.
Your brain *best* connects the good feeling of the reward to your behavior if the reward takes place during or immediately after the action. If you can only reward at a later time you will have to make sure that you clearly keep the link in mind between your behavior and the reward. Play the movie of what you did in your mind and reward yourself on the basis of this.

It is of the utmost importance that we find the right reward or motivator for ourselves. And once again: often we have to support the original motivation (which is aimed at the *ultimate goal*) with a large amount of temporary 'artificial' motivation (which stimulates related *behavior*).
It helps to explicitly think of your ultimate goal during and immediately after the behavior. But adding a few extra boosts, for example in the form of material rewards, is often necessary.

A few examples:
- When you have replaced all of your snacks by mineral water on the first day of your healthier way of life you are allowed to rent a nice DVD that evening.
- When you have managed to approach your colleagues in a positive way and with a lot of patience on the first day it is time for a relaxing evening with a new book.
- When you have studied the first chapter of your study book it is time for a break and a snack.

It is sometimes very difficult to choose the right motivators and rewards. On the basis of the experience we have gained and the beliefs this has given us, we all have our own perspective of the world. What exactly we regard as a punishment or as a reward is also determined by this. This can cause matters to be motivating for one person, but completely demotivating for somebody else. This means that there are no universal rules for rewarding.

Apart from this some rewards counteract our goals in the long run. Somebody who wants to live a healthier life and stops smoking but is crazy about chocolate will first of all think of a nice bar of Swiss chocolate as a reward. But after a year the next problem presents itself: overweight.

A change coach

In the previous chapter we shortly discussed this aspect. You often need the support of others in your environment for your most important changes. These can be people from your direct environment, like your partner or a good friend. It is good in any case to involve them in a major change.

But it can sometimes also be useful to find a real coach. Somebody you choose especially for this process and may even pay for the work he or she does.

Coaching and other forms of social support – even if this is just one phone call per week from somebody else – prove to be an important factor for success in change processes.

A coach watching over your shoulder works as an important incentive

Coaches can play a part in the starting phase: the dream and the dare phase in which you sometimes will need a sounding board. But in the do phase they can play an important role in the actual persistence. The encouragement of another person when going through a change is experienced as very motivating by almost anybody.

And the knowledge that somebody will ask you how things go every now and again works as an important incentive for many people. Measuring and rewarding takes place much more conscientiously when a coach is watching over your shoulder.

It is important to determine beforehand what type of coach you are looking for.

- *Are you looking for a good listener*: somebody who asks questions and makes you think; who does not judge but mainly serves as a sounding board?
- *Are you looking for a 'fellow-changer' or partner*: somebody who also wants to change something and so not only listens but also expects you to listen actively?
- *Or are you looking for a mentor:* somebody with knowledge about the change you want and who can coach you optimally?

In addition to this it is of vital importance that you trust the other person. If you use a listener as a coach you have to make sure that he or she is genuinely interested in you. If you talk to a 'fellow-changer' you have to be sure that his or her situation is more or less comparable to yours. And if you have a mentor you need to be convinced of his or her expertise and professionalism.

Avoid postponement

In the 'Dare' chapters I have told you that doing something new for the first time also forms the first moment of crisis for most people. We can be very reluctant to make a start with a change, so much so that we'd rather postpone beginning. Many people don't consciously give up important changes. They just postpone starting the change so long that they never get around to doing it.

Why do we postpone things? There are two reasons:

- *We are afraid of the short-term frustrations that our new behavior can give us*. We may have experienced in the past that our intention causes pain especially at the beginning. We may be too much of a perfectionist and can't live with the fact that new things don't immediately go right. Whatever the case, we'd rather stay in our comfort zone for a while.
- *We 'enjoy' the pressure which the postponement gives us*. Some people enjoy arriving at the platform just in time to jump on the train. It is the relief of just escaping the 'imminent punishment'. If these are things you do regularly you can get away with it. But if it is something new, it is an unwise strategy. You simply don't have enough experience with your new behavior yet to be able to estimate correctly whether you are able to make it.

The solution is obvious and equivalent to the means I advised you for crisis situations.
Prepare the first day thoroughly with reminders, rewards and counter behavior. If necessary turn this day into a real festive day: celebrate such a first day. Allow yourself some space as well to concentrate on your change and do not try to do it on the side.

- If you stop smoking, make it a relaxing day. Watch nice movies in bed.

- If you start exercising, treat yourself to a long, relaxing bath afterwards.
- If you take an important step in your relationship, go out in the evening and take the next morning off.

And – this is important – realize that some insecurity is part of life. Also famous and experienced artists are nervous on the evening of the premiere of a new play.

Dream, Dare, Do ...

- People mainly learn by immediate feedback. This means that we need to measure and reward the desired behavior from the very start.
- Many people benefit from a change coach in this phase. They want to get feedback from somebody else and need an extra incentive.
- We can avoid postponement by preparing the start thoroughly. If it is not automatically fun to start, make it fun.

'There is no medicine and it can't be cured'

Jane (43) is married to Edward. She is the mother of three sons and she is chronically ill.
Nine years ago it started when one of her toes died off, and the next winter another one. 'After I had been through all the tests, it turned out that I suffered from cryoglobulinemia. That means that my blood clots below 16 degrees Celsius. The trouble is that there is no medicine for this and it can't be cured. It can only be stopped by warmth. Also my stomach and intestines are affected and I have had several heart attacks and small strokes.'
Jane can't go outside in winter. She is on a strict diet and is always in pain.

At the beginning she didn't realize the impact this would have. 'I thought if I could go out in summer, I could still do a lot of things.' Until winter came and she realized she couldn't go out anymore. She started to feel an outsider and that she was not involved in the daily run of things anymore.
'I had always been active: I attended a sewing class, did a lot of volunteer work in church and at my sons' school. But those kinds of things usually take place in the winter.
I couldn't even go out when I was restless and that very much confronted me with myself and my illness. I first kept to bed for a whole week and didn't want to talk to anybody. I had completely lost myself.'

'After that week I thought: "I can do two things. Either I can keep to myself completely and become deeply unhappy, and so would my family. Or I am going to try and find my peace of mind again and start afresh from there."
I chose the latter and first wrote everything down. I wrote down what bothered me because my body didn't cooperate anymore. With Edward, my doctor and a good friend, I talked a lot and realized that my situation is the way it is and will not change.'

'I always made myself do so many things'

'Step by step I found a rhythm again with small things and started finding my limits. I started looking for alternatives for the things I can't do anymore. For example, I now read children's books because I sometimes

mix up words; I started doing things which can be done inside, like making cards and embroidering. And I invite people at home.
At the beginning I had to do my utmost for the things I changed, but at a certain point these became natural. '

It was difficult to adapt her expectations and those of others. Jane was used to getting her energy and approval from things she did for others.
'I thought you could only get recognition for things others see the result of. For example, I always cleaned my home thoroughly and always said I liked that. But in fact I don't like it at all. When I first couldn't do that anymore, I had to let it go. I was afraid my mother would say it was not clean enough.
One day I just said that out loud. My friends now say that I give so much by just being there. At first I couldn't imagine that to be true. I really had to start believing in myself again.'

'I can enjoy life much more now. I very much enjoy the company of friends who visit. I can relax more now, while earlier I often thought: *yes, I am here now, sitting and drinking coffee, but I need to clean the bathroom later.*
Since I fell ill the moments of joy are really priceless. The joy of my family, music, friends.
If I had just continued the life I lived I wouldn't have been so happy. Then I would always have been busy and out a lot. I always made myself do so many things.
Now I think: what do others miss much because they are always trying to perform. Maybe it is easier to just let go when you are forced to.'

Dream, Dare, Do...

- Some things are difficult to accept and can't be changed. You can give up or rethink from a perspective of the possibilities that remain.
- If we don't think in terms of succeeding and failing, but in terms of learning, unpleasant incidents will also make us stronger and wiser.
- Do not let your life be determined by what you think others expect from you. But talk about it with them and dare to make your own choices.

10 Do: finishing with persistence

- ***If everything is a learning process, failure does not exist anymore***
- ***But what do we do in a case of relapse?***
- ***Dream, dare, do as second nature***

In the previous chapter I told you about my daughter Emma and her ambition to learn to ride a bike. Suppose that I had not succeeded in teaching her how to ride a bike the first time. We practised all afternoon, but it just didn't work. How many times do I try again to teach her this? How long would you continue if you want to teach a child to ride a bike?

Of course, until she is able to ride it!

With all things we really find important in life we continue until we master them. Small children often fall down many times when they learn to walk but there isn't any parent who would say: 'You've fallen down ten times now, let's stop. Tough luck, too bad. You failed. It is not going to work for you. Apparently you are not a walker. You are more of a crawler.'

'It is not going to work for you. Apparently you are not a walker. You are more of a crawler.'

And what do people do who have an accident or an illness which causes them to be unable to walk temporarily? They start convalescing and learn anew, if need be with some sort of aid. And if walking isn't possible anymore they learn to move independently in a wheelchair. For all things we genuinely find worthwhile we continue until we have reach our goal one way or another.

Each step in the change process is a test for your motivation. Each step gives you more grip on your own behavior but meanwhile also demands attention, time and energy. Only if you find a change really important, will you put that effort in. You may come to the conclusion while reading these final chapters that you are not prepared to make all this effort.
That is no shame but a healthy cost-benefit analysis, as long as you make your decision honestly and voluntarily!

If you, however, have decided to *persist*, if you really want to turn your ambition into action and result, do yourself a favor and forget thinking in terms of succeeding and failing. Failure does not exist if you intend to continue. At the most you can learn and do it better next time.

Our life as a learning process
I indicated earlier that it is important to experiment. Every now and then try out something new. Think up a surprise for your partner; choose a short course to do; rent a movie which you would not normally choose; talk to other people on the train; call somebody tonight whom you haven't talked to for a long time, somebody you may have to make amends to.....

Act out of character once in a while and go to the borders of your YES area. Find out if you can stretch your borders a bit. In this way you develop yourself. It makes life fun and gives self-confidence. In addition to this you get used to the tingling in your stomach which you feel when doing these kinds of new activities.

Everything goes, as long as you consider it an experiment, a way to learn something. If you see your attempt to change as an experiment, failure does not exist anymore. The fact is an experiment always yields results. You learn how you should not do it, or you learn how you should do it.

Find out if you can stretch the borders of your YES area

For that matter, it is true that experimenting often also is a good way to win over other people in a change. Of course, this is not the core topic of this book but in many cases other people are involved. Our partner, our colleagues, friends, family.
If you ask them to cooperate in a change and you present it as something which is ambitious, irreversible and comprehensive, the chance isn't so large that you make them enthusiastic immediately. But think in terms of small experiments and you will encounter less resistance. Logically, there is little to be lost and a lot to be gained.

Looking at a personal change from a perspective of 'succeeding and failing' might just be the most ineffective thing you can do. Life is all about learning. Once you have got that into to your skull everything becomes much more interesting and much more fun.

Continuous measuring and rewarding?
When you start changing, daily measuring and rewarding are very important. But how long do we need to continue? Do we have to keep measuring *forever* and do we have to keep rewarding *forever*?

Let's discuss rewarding first. Once you have found the right behavior a natural reward will follow it, often after some time. Your relationship improves, you feel better, you feel healthier, you see results in your work. Sometimes this only takes a few days but often it takes weeks or even months before we see real results when making major changes.

My advice is to enjoy these 'natural' results consciously. Regularly repeat to yourself that this is the reward for the choice to manage yourself better.
Meanwhile you can reduce other 'artificial' rewards step by step. You can also choose not to reward yourself each time but only every second or third time that you execute your intended behavior. You can also postpone your reward longer and longer.

Often it takes weeks or even months before we see real results

And how about measuring? In any case you will have to keep measuring your behavior as long as you still work with artificial rewards. Otherwise you can't determine when you are entitled to it.
But even when you have completely switched to enjoying your natural rewards it is still good to continue measuring. In this way you create a moment at which you consciously reflect on your own performances.
In the long run this frequency can be decreased. You do not measure daily anymore, but weekly or monthly. Stopping measuring completely, however, isn't very smart. Your old behavior in which you felt really well once is still there in your MP3 player in your mind and can always crop up again. Often this old behavior will take control imperceptibly; so make sure that you keep checking every now and again.

Coping with relapse
Despite our precautions we may all have to deal with relapse. After a tiring day you do get angry again with your partner. After a disappointing night out you relapse into self-pity again. And when your friends cancel dinner at the last moment you do plunder the fridge again.

Old automatic feelings, thoughts and actions always stay in our MP3 player. And when the wrong buttons are pushed at an unexpected moment we can sometimes relapse after many years.
These things happen. Oh well, too bad. More important is the question how you deal with it! *Do not be annoyed but be amazed* my sister used to say. Anger and sadness don't help, curiosity does. What do you learn from this? What action is required in these kinds of situations?

If you can see relapse as learning experience there is no problem. It may be annoying, and you make it more difficult on yourself to persist. That's right. But you have learned something again as well. You have familiarized yourself with an extra crisis situation which will not surprise you anymore next time.
If you walk up the stairs at home and trip over a stair which is loose you don't stay downstairs for the rest of your life, do you? Next time you are extra careful at that one stair.

Do not pity or punish yourself extremely after a relapse into old bad habits. And do not justify your behavior. In both cases you take the step to a next relapse, and another one and yet another one, as easy as that. It will not take long before you will have to conclude that none of your efforts have been of any use.

Persisting and renewing
Important changes are always on-going. Whoever has been addicted to smoking, drinking, gambling or other stimulants knows this. Relapse always lies in wait. Also after many years.
Breaking ineffective habits and learning new effective habits is never completely 'finished'. It is important to keep checking yourself and reminding yourself of the result which you have reached with a lot of pain and effort.

In some cases you will never be free of measuring. You will have to keep checking the state of affairs regularly for the rest of your life to determine whether you are still on track.
Some years ago I still believed that I really could do everything on willpower. Meanwhile, now that I am older and wiser, I have worked with a list of behavior for some years. One month I use it a bit more

When I notice that certain good habits are in danger of disappearing again I will bring out my list again

disciplined than another. But when I notice that certain good habits are in danger of disappearing again I will bring out my list and have a look at it again.

I renew my list at least twice a year. I ask myself if my long-term goals are still right (usually they are). And I check whether the intentions on my list are still useful and feasible. Do they still match my goals? And will I manage to bring them into practice?
In this way I have already adapted my daily physical exercises several times. Often it turns out that I have made it too complicated for myself – instead of ten minutes a day it suddenly costs me twenty minutes a day – and I have to simplify my list again.

In fact I go through the three steps – dream, dare, do – a few times per year. What once started as a powerful aid for a few changes has become an effective way to manage myself better.

Dream, dare, do as a permanent habit
Whoever has made a change in his life often gets the hang of it. A successful change gives self-confidence and gives the motivation to continue and set new goals.
You can also feel the need to help other people with their attempts to change. To share your experience and insights with somebody who is still before a change.
The three steps which are at the center of this book – dream, dare, do – can help you with this. They play an essential role in each change.
That is why it is worthwhile to master these three steps.

Dream... It is a good habit to consciously look for possibilities of growth and improvement in your YES area regularly. And by formulating goal-oriented and concrete behavioral intentions you increase the chance to bring your intentions into practice enormously.

Dare... It is a good habit to go through possible crisis situations in advance and think up strategies to persevere no matter what. This decreases the chance of relapse and also stimulates the courage to start difficult things.

Do...It is a good habit to measure and reward new, desired behavior. For yourself, but also for others. In addition, working with rewards instead of threats or punishment has a positive influence on your relations with others.

These are universal principles in the field of change which are directly related to basic human characteristics. You can apply them to yourself, but also in raising children, in educational situations, in communication with friends and colleagues, in running companies.... In fact in all goal-oriented forms of change we can think of.

By practising these principles you will learn how you can learn more effectively. This is useful for the rest of your life.

Dream, Dare, Do ...

- Do not think in terms of succeeding or failing, but in terms of learning. If you really think your goals are important, you can't fail but you can only learn as you go.
- We will often have to keep measuring our behavior for a longer period to form new behaviors and to prevent relapse. A year or longer is no exception.
- Successful changes work as a stimulator. Whoever turns the three steps *dream, dare* and *do* into habits will get more grip on his life.

Epilogue

The approach I have described in this book is not a religion or philosophy. It is a practical aid to live in a constructive, future-oriented way based on your most important beliefs, an aid to not get carried away by each external influence, but to lead your own life.

Just to be clear, I don't believe that life is makable. Most things happening around us can't be managed. We will encounter illness, accidents, and death in our lives. That isn't very nice, but it is the reality of life.
At the most we can control part of our behavior and the way we deal with the inevitable.

I look at myself more modestly, and see others more sympathetically and more compassionately

The latter, dealing with setbacks, is a skill which is essential to be able to lead a normal life. Whoever expects life to be nothing but prosperity and happiness or that a life like that is on command, will certainly be disappointed.

And I hope that you can use the contents of this book to your advantage in several ways.
First of all, you will notice that you have more control of your own behavior if you follow up the advice in this book.

Besides, you will understand more of your own behavior and that of others. That's also a positive thing.

By learning more about behavior in the past years, I have learned to look at myself more modestly, and see others more sympathetically and more compassionately. And that in itself is pure gain.

Ben Tiggelaar

Dream, Dare, Do test

How good are you at changing? How effectively do you usually control your own behavior? Take the test and discover what you are good at and what you can do better.

The test consists of twelve questions. Circle the answer that suits you best. Fill out the answers as realistically as possible.

Dream

1. **When I have a certain wish I wonder what it would *feel* like if this wish came true.**

   never – sometimes – regularly – often – always

2. **When changing I tend to *first* focus on the things I am not able to do (yet)**

   never – sometimes – regularly – often – always

3. **When I want something I try to imagine the final result as *clearly and concretely* as possible.**

   never – sometimes – regularly – often – always

4. **When I know which result I am reaching for I determine very clearly what *I* have to *do* for it.**

   never – sometimes – regularly – often – always

Dare

5. **When I know what I want to change I consider the *difficult situations* which could form an obstacle for my intention beforehand.**

   never – sometimes – regularly – often – always

6. **When I know which things can form an obstacle I think of all kinds of ways to *persevere no matter what*.**

   never – sometimes – regularly – often – always

7. **When I want to change something in my life I make a *step by step plan.***
never – sometimes – regularly – often – always

8. **When I really intend to change something I look for *somebody else* to support me in this process.**

never – sometimes – regularly – often – always

Do

9. **When I am in the process of changing I *remind* myself regularly why it was I wanted to change.**

never – sometimes – regularly – often – always

10. **When I am in the process of changing I *measure meticulously* whether I succeed in sticking to my intentions.**

never – sometimes – regularly – often – always

11. **When I stick to my intentions during my process of change I *reward myself.***

never – sometimes – regularly – often – always

12. **Also after I have completed a major change I *check* regularly whether I am still on track.**

never – sometimes – regularly – often – always

Scores and explanation
Below you will find how many points you can score for each answer. Add the points per phase (dream, dare, do). With each phase you will find an explanation and a few tips.

Dream

Question 1: never (0) – sometimes (1) – regularly (2) – often (3) – always (4)
Question 2: never (4) – sometimes (3) – regularly (2) – often (1) – always (0)
Question 3: never (0) – sometimes (1) – regularly (2) – often (3) – always (4)
Question 4: never (0) – sometimes (2) – regularly (4) – often (6) – always (8)

Fewer than 12 points in this part
Everyone has dreams about the future. One way of dreaming is much more effective than another. If you have a clear picture of which direction you want to go, the chance is bigger that you will realize (part of) your dreams.
It is especially important to translate your dreams subsequently into behavior. What are you going to do to reach your goals? Which goal-oriented and feasible new habits help you to go into the direction you have chosen?
In chapters five and six it is explained how you determine your direction and how you translate this into every day action.

More than 12 points in this part
You probably have a good picture of what you want. That is a good start. Do take into account that setting clear goals alone often isn't sufficient. It is important to translate them into concrete behavior. What exactly are you going to do, every day, to make your dreams really come true? Which new habits are necessary for this?
In chapters five and six you will probably find a number of things you already do regularly. Next to these, you will familiarize yourself with a number of insights and techniques which help you to formulate your wishes even more effectively.

Dare

Question 5: never (0) – sometimes (1) – regularly (2) – often (3) – always (4)
Question 6: never (0) – sometimes (2) – regularly (4) – often (6) – always (8)
Question 7: never (0) – sometimes (1) – regularly (2) – often (3) – always (4)
Question 8: never (0) – sometimes (1) – regularly (2) – often (3) – always (4)

Fewer than 12 points in this part
There is a possibility that many of your attempts to change in the past have failed, maybe immediately at the beginning and otherwise during a moment of crisis on the way. Many people know that there will be difficult moments during personal processes of change, but still they don't take the right precautions. This almost always causes them to relapse into old habits they want to get rid of.
In chapters seven and eight you will find a number of tips to spot the obstacles in advance and techniques to eliminate them and persevere.

More than 12 points in this part
You already deal with changes in your life quite proficiently. In any case you know that it will not always be easy during the process and you prepare for that. Very sensible.
And so in chapters seven and eight you will find a few familiar matters. Besides, in chapter eight especially, you will find a number of techniques which will help you to even better persevere at difficult moments. The chance of changing successfully increases by at least a factor three to four when you use them.

Do

Question 9: never (0) – sometimes (1) – regularly (2) – often (3) – always (4)
Question 10: never (0) – sometimes (2) – regularly (4) – often (6) – always (8)
Question 11: never (0) – sometimes (1) – regularly (2) – often (3) – always (4)
Question 12: never (0) – sometimes (1) – regularly (2) – often (3) – always (4)

Fewer than 12 points in this part
Preparing yourself for a change is a lot of work. But finally what it comes down to is whether you really come into action and continue. Behavior is the weak link between plans and results.
Often it is necessary to remind yourself regularly of the 'why' for your change. Why do you do all this?
Feedback is at least as important: Do you really do what is necessary? Measuring your behavior daily and rewarding yourself are two powerful techniques to start changing and persevering. In chapters nine and ten you will read more about this.

More than 12 points in this part
You already understand very well what it takes to control your own behavior. You remind yourself regularly of the 'why' of your actions; you keep track of your own behavior and reward yourself; you do not think too quickly that you are 'ready' changing. My compliments.
In chapters nine and ten you will find a few more insights and techniques which will help you to control your daily actions consciously. If you are capable of turning the approach in these chapters into one of your habits, you will be able to manage yourself more and more effectively.

Literature

The most important books and articles used in this book:

- Ajzen, I. (1991). The theory of planned behavior. Organizational behavior and human decision processes, 50, 179-211.

- Bandura, A. & Locke, E.A. (2003). Negative Self-Efficacy and Goal Effects Revisited. In: Journal of Applied Psychology, 88, 87-99. American Psychological Association.

- Bargh, J.A. & Chartrand, T. (1999). The Unbearable Automaticity of Being. In: American Psychologist, 57, 705-717. American Psychological Association.

- Grant, L., & Evans, A. (1994). Principles of behavior analysis. New York: Harper Collins.

- Gollwitzer, P.M. (1999), Implementation Intentions. Strong Effects of Simple Plans, in: American Psychologist, 54, 493-503. American Psychological Association.

- Hassin, R.R., Uleman, J.S., & Bargh, J.A. (Eds.) (2005) The New Unconscious. New York: Oxford University Press.

- Locke, E.A. & Latham, G.P. (2002). Building a Practically Useful Theory of Goal Setting and Task Motivation, in: American Psychologist, 57, 705-717. American Psychological Association.

- Muraven, M.; Tice, D.M. & Baumeister, R.E. (1998). Self-Control as Limited Resource: Regulatory Depletion Patterns, in: Journal of Personality and Social Psychology. 74, 774-789. American Psychological Association.

- Ouellette, J.A. & Wood, W. (1998), Habit and Intention in Everyday Life: The Multiple Processes by which Past Behavior Predicts Future Behavior, Psychological Bulletin, 124, 54-74.

- Perugini, M. & Bagozzi, R.P. (2001). The role of desires and anticipated emotions in goal-directed behaviours: Broadening and deepening the theory of planned behaviour. In: British Journal of Social Psychology, 40, 79-98. British Psychological Society.

- Peterson, C., & Seligman, M.E.P. (2004). Character strengths and virtues: A handbook and classification. Washington, DC: American Psychological Association.

- Prochaska, J.O., DiClemente, C.C. & Norcross, J.C. (1992). In Search of How People Change. Applications to Addictive Behaviors. In: American Psychologist, 47, 1102-1114. American Psychological Association

- Prochaska, J.O., DiClemente, C.C. & Norcross, J.C. (1994). Changing for Good. New York: Avon Books.

- Sarafino, E.P. (1996). Principles of Behavior Change. New York: John Wiley & Sons.

- Seligman, M.E.P. (1994). What You Can Change and What You Can't. New York: Knopf.

- Seligman, M.E.P. (2002). Authentic Happiness. New York: Free Press.

- Seligman, M.E.P., & Csikszentmihalyi, M. (2000). Positive Psychology: An Introduction. American Psychologist, 55, 5-14. American Psychological Association.

- Seligman, M.E.P., Steen, T.A., Park, N. & Peterson, C. (2005). Positive Psychology Progress. Empirical Validation of Interventions. American Psychologist, 60, 410-421. American Psychological Association.

- Wilson, T.D. (2002). Strangers to ourselves: Discovering the adaptive unconscious. Cambridge, MA: Harvard University Press.

About Ben Tiggelaar

Ben Tiggelaar (1969) is a husband and a father. Next to that he is a researcher and author in the field of leadership, change and behavior.

He is known as one of the absolute top speakers and trainers in his field of expertise.

Ben wrote several books on management and change, including his best seller CAN DO!.

For up-to-date information and additions to this book please check his website on www.tiggelaar.com